1 0 MAY 2007

Return this item by
the last date shown.

Items may be renewed
by telephone or at
www.eastrenfrewshire.gov.uk/libraries

Bad Hair Day
A guide to female hair loss

Francesca Collins,
Sebastiana Biondo and
Rodney Sinclair

Lothian
BOOKS

EAST RENFREWSHIRE COUNCIL	
0564073	
Bertrams	17.02.07
616.546	£7.99

Thomas C. Lothian Pty Ltd
132 Albert Road, South Melbourne, Victoria 3205
www.lothian.com.au

Copyright © Francesca Collins,
Sebastiana Biondo and Rodney Sinclair 2005

First published 2005

All rights reserved. No part of this publication may be reproduced, stored in a retrieval system or transmitted in any form by any means without the prior permission of the copyright owner. Enquiries should be made to the publisher.

National Library of Australia
Cataloguing-in-Publication data:

Collins, Francesca.
  Bad hair day.

  0 7344 0902 8

  1. Baldness. 2. Women — Health and hygiene.
  I. Biondo, Sebastiana. II. Sinclair, Rodney. III. Title.

A823.3

Cover design by Christa Moffitt, Christabella Designs
Text design by Paulene Meyer
Printed in Australia by Griffin Press

Contents

Authors' biographical notes		7
Introduction		11
1	What's happening to my hair?	13
2	The root of the problem	23
3	Genes and hormones	31
4	The impact of hair loss	39
5	Thoughts, feelings and coping	55
6	Styling, camouflaging and replacing	83
7	Myths and medical treatments	105
8	Planning and patience	125
Techniques for relaxation		135
Useful resources		147
The Halo Program		153

Authors' biographical notes

Francesca Collins BA, BSc (Hons), PhD, MAPS

Dr Collins is a lecturer in Behavioural Studies at Monash University and has a private practice as a psychological consultant. She is the founder and convenor of Dissociation Australia, the Australian branch of the International Society for the Study of Dissociation, and co-author and facilitator of the Halo Program, a group therapy program for women with female pattern hair loss at the Alfred Hospital. Dr Collins has published widely in the areas of female hair loss, dissociation and higher education.

SEBASTIANA BIONDO BSc, GRADDIP (PSYCH), MPSYCH, ASSOC MAPS

Sebastiana Biondo is an academic in Behavioural Studies at Monash University where she teaches and conducts research into the psychological impact of female pattern hair loss. She is co-author and facilitator of the Halo Program, has published internationally in the area of female hair loss, and provides psychological consulting at the Skin and Cancer Foundation of Victoria. She is a committee member of the Alopecia Support Association.

RODNEY SINCLAIR MBBS, MD, FACD

Professor Rodney Sinclair is Professor of Dermatology at the University of Melbourne, Director of Dermatology at St Vincent's Hospital and Director of Research and Training at the Skin and Cancer Foundation. He is immediate Past President of the Skin and Cancer Foundation of Victoria and President Elect of the Australasian Society for Dermatology Research. He is a founding member and Past President of the Australasian Hair and Wool Research Society. Professor Sinclair is the co-author of a section on dermatology in the *Oxford Textbook of Medicine* and chapter on hair disorders in Rook's *Textbook of Dermatology*. He has written seven dermatology textbooks, over 150 journal articles and has contributed more than fifty book chapters. He is recognised internationally for his work on female pattern hair loss.

Introduction

If a doctor has just diagnosed you with female pattern hair loss, also known as androgenetic alopecia, you're probably feeling angry, sad, and above all, shocked. These feelings are completely normal and will probably last a while. It might even be a few weeks before you feel ready to read this book.

If you received your diagnosis some time ago, you may have spent many hours searching for reliable information about the condition and its treatment. Our aim is to provide you with all the information, treatment tips and grooming techniques you need to live confidently. In this book you'll find out about:

- ✂ what hair is and why we have it
- ✂ the causes and course of female pattern hair loss

- ✂ medical and cosmetic treatments
- ✂ how to manage the psychological impact of hair loss
- ✂ help for hair styling, hair pieces and camouflage
- ✂ the truth behind many hair myths and quack cures
- ✂ women's personal accounts and experiences

Besides supporting you, this book will help your friends, family, hairdressers and health professionals understand your condition better. A condition that affects one in five women over thirty, and one in two women over sixty.

FRANCESCA COLLINS BA, BSc (HONS), PhD, MAPS

SEBASTIANA BIONDO BSc, GRADDIP (PSYCH), MPSYCH, ASSOC, MAPS

RODNEY SINCLAIR MBBS, MD, FACD

1
What's happening to my hair?

Balding in men is so common it doesn't raise an eyebrow. But when a woman starts to lose hair she finds it extremely distressing. Her locks are her crowning glory. Will she end up bald, too? The first port of call is her hairdresser or doctor.

HELP! I'VE GOT ALOPECIA!

The term *alopecia* means baldness. Nothing more, nothing less. Alopecia on its own doesn't describe the type or the cause of a particular sort of hair loss. And women can lose significant amounts of hair for a number of very different reasons.

Everyone knows chemotherapy can make hair

fall out. But after the medical treatment hair will grow again. Similarly, hair over the entire scalp can be shed because of other medications, pregnancy, thyroid disorders, major surgery, fever, blood loss, iron deficiency, starvation and crash dieting. This diffuse hair loss is the not uncommon, and usually temporary, condition called *telogen effluvium.* The shedding can last two or three months before the woman recovers completely, although occasionally it can become chronic. Then there's alopecia areata, an autoimmune condition said to have affected Marie Antoinette, where clumps of hair fall out and leave bald patches.

Female pattern hair loss (FPHL) is quite distinct from all these types of hair loss. It is a genetic condition, and fifty per cent of women are predisposed to it. Some of these women will be affected almost as soon as they reach puberty, while others may remain unaffected until after menopause. The course of FPHL differs from woman to woman, however once it starts it will continue, and each year an additional five to ten per cent of hair may be lost from the affected areas of the scalp. And as if it isn't bad enough suffering from FPHL, these women can also experience occasional diffuse hair loss.

An additional problem for many women is to find how little hair and health professionals know about a condition that affects one in five women over the age of thirty, and one in two over sixty. Initial visits may result in comments such as, 'It's just stress/pregnancy/the weather — it'll grow back.' Or, 'Well, at least you don't have a fatal disease.' Or, 'You're imagining things! You have plenty of hair.'

It can be crushing to have worked up the courage to seek help, only to be told you are over-reacting. But this situation is changing as the condition becomes better understood by professionals and effective treatments are developed. Don't give up! Research shows women don't overstate their hair loss, as a rule. If anything, they tend to perceive it as less severe than it really is.

Female pattern hair loss is very common. Fewer than half of all women go through life without losing some hair due to it.

WHAT DOES FPHL LOOK LIKE?

Female pattern hair loss begins with diffuse thinning over the top and front parts of the scalp, most noticeably in the centre. While the hair loss is most pronounced on the crown, it can also be thinned from ear to ear. The back of the head is least affected. This particular pattern of hair loss is distinctive and unique to FPHL.

DIAGNOSIS

Most women affected by FPHL notice increased hair shedding before they become aware of a loss of hair volume over the crown. Others don't notice their hair shedding, yet see their hair has reduced in volume, has less body and has become more difficult to manage. Women who have long hair may notice their ponytail becoming thinner.

At first the shedding or thinning occurs in fits and bursts. Episodes may last anywhere between three and six months and may then abate for one to two years before recurring. Over time, the episodes occur progressively closer together, until some women find they are shedding all year round.

Doctors not trained in hair loss conditions may find it difficult to diagnose FPHL as there is no clear definition of what's normal. For most women, a daily loss of between 50 and 150 hairs is normal;

this normal range may extend to 200 hairs per day for women with particularly dense hair. For most women, shedding more than two hundred hairs per day is unusual. Whether you normally lose 50 or 150 per day is not so important; what *is* important is a *change* in your usual amount of shedding. Most women have a clear idea of what is normal for them, and a deviation in what they consider normal may indicate a problem. For some women, shedding as few as thirty hairs a day will be abnormal.

When someone notices an increase in shedding, it may be due either to a true increase in the number of hairs coming out, or to an increased interest in catching and counting the number of shed hairs. This is not the strange activity it may at first seem — many people in the early stages of hair loss track the progress of their condition by keeping and counting their fallen hairs. Shedding that stops and starts just adds to the confusion.

Professor Rodney Sinclair has developed a clinical grading scale — the **Sinclair Scale** — to help doctors diagnose FPHL. The scale grades FPHL into five stages of hair loss.

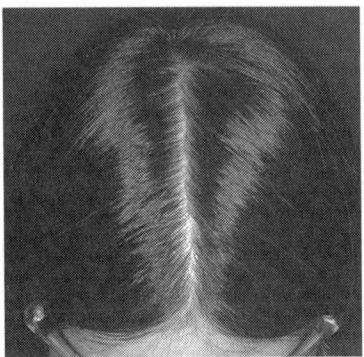

Grade 1 is normal. This pattern is found in all girls prior to puberty but in only forty-five per cent of women aged eighty and over.

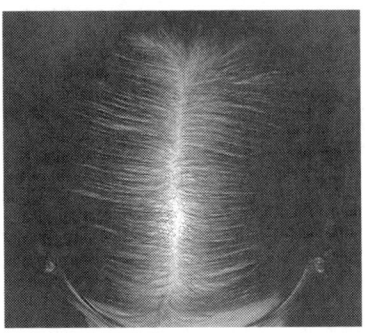

Grade 2 shows a widening of the central part.

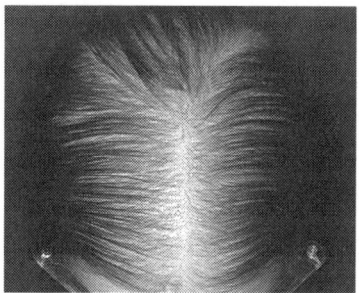

Grade 3 shows a widening of the central part and thinning of the hair on either side of the part line.

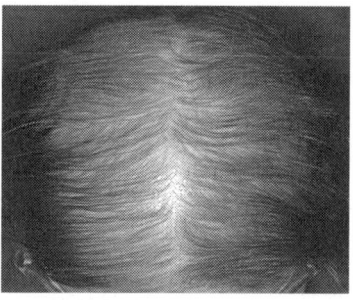

Grade 4 reveals the emergence of a diffuse hair loss over the top of the scalp.

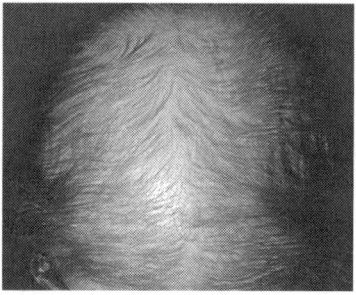

Grade 5 indicates advanced hair loss.

It is important to note that even in advanced FPHL, the affected area does not become completely bald and the hairline is always retained. In contrast, a receding hair line at the temples (bi-temporal recession) is seen in about two thirds of all women and is considered normal. This bi-temporal recession is generally mild with fewer than ten per cent of women having deep bi-temporal recession. The presence and depth of recession at the temples is not related to FPHL — many women get one without the other.

Women with advanced hair thinning (Grade 2 or higher) may never have been aware of increased hair shedding; for this group, the grading scale alone is sufficient to diagnose FPHL. Some women, however, will have experienced hair shedding for six or more months, but still have a normal hair pattern (Grade 1). Women in this group will usually require additional tests, including a scalp biopsy.

SCALP BIOPSY

For women who are experiencing increased hair shedding but, to the outside observer, appear to have no visible hair loss, the most useful diagnostic test is a scalp biopsy. It's helpful for women with normal hair density when:

- ✂ increased hair shedding has been present for more than six months
- ✂ increased hair shedding is occurring without an obvious alternate explanation
- ✂ there are multiple relapsing episodes — each less than six months — of increased hair shedding
- ✂ an incomplete recovery follows an acute episode of increased hair shedding.

A scalp biopsy is a minor surgical procedure conducted under local anaesthetic in your doctor's office. The doctor will remove one or more tiny plugs of tissue from your scalp, about four millimetres in diameter. These plugs are sent to a pathologist who will determine whether there is evidence of FPHL and, to some extent, how much hair has already been lost. Because the scalp has a rich blood supply, a stitch is required to stop the bleeding and encourage healing. It brings the edges of skin together and can be painlessly removed after a week. The only scar is a small faint line. Without a stitch the biopsy scar would leave a small bald spot.

Some women experience a headache for a few hours after their scalp biopsy, but most find it no more troublesome than a blood test.

2
The root of the problem

When a doctor diagnoses you with FPHL you can rest assured nothing — absolutely nothing — you've done to your hair or scalp has caused it. You can forget past beauty treatments because waxing, gelling, colouring, perming, blow-drying, frequent hair washing (or no washing at all) are not the culprits. Nor are the environment, diet, emotional factors, stress or hats — they all have little or no role in the development of FPHL. In short, don't blame yourself, because it's not your fault.

While you're concerned about the appearance of the hair you can see, it's what you can't see that's governing your hair loss.

Hair grows from hair follicles — minute,

sock-like indentations in the skin. Everyone's born with more than two million of them over their entire body, including around a hundred thousand on the scalp. No new follicles develop after birth — in fact we lose a small number each year as we age, but each one will produce a number of hairs during the course of our lives. These follicles are where all the action — or inaction — takes place. In fact, the lower part of a follicle is the only section where hair is alive.

Most of the hairs on our face and body are tiny. These fine, short, barely visible hairs are vellus hairs, while the longer, thicker, pigmented hairs found on the scalp, eyebrows and eyelashes are terminal hairs.

At puberty most male mammals, but not female mammals, grow hair over certain parts of their body. The mane of the adult male lion is an example. In humans, however, both males and females grow coarse hairs on the pubic region, underarms and legs, while only boys grow beards and chest hair.

In contrast, some mammals *lose* hair with sexual maturity. The male stump-tailed macaque monkey goes bald over the top of the scalp after puberty.

However, male and female humans are the only mammals that both grow hair in some places *and* lose it in others with puberty.

THE HAIR CYCLE

Have you ever wondered why people's pubic hair doesn't sweep the floor as they walk? Or, if they don't shave under their arms, why the hair from their armpits doesn't peep out from their shirt-sleeves?

Hair grows at a rate of about one centimetre a month, which is why most people get a haircut every six to eight weeks. This *rate* of hair growth is much the same over the entire body, so that if you were to shave your scalp, eyebrows and armpits at the same time they would all regrow at the same speed. But the duration of hair growth is different on different parts of our body. That is, non-scalp hair, such as armpit hair, may grow for only five months before falling out whereas scalp hair can continue to grow for as long as seven years. It is this variation in the duration of hair growth — not in the rate of hair growth — that produces hairs of different length on our scalp and elsewhere on our bodies. It is a result of the body's hormonal regulation of the hair growth cycle.

Every hair on our head is at a different stage in the hair cycle, either growing, dying, resting or regrowing. This is where we differ from animals that adapt to the seasons and moult. Their hairs are all in the same stages of the cycle at the same time which means all their long winter hairs fall out in spring to be replaced with new, short hairs for summer.

Fortunately we humans don't rely on our hair for temperature regulation. We don't shed every single hair on our head or body in the space of a few weeks. Instead we tend to lose a relatively small number each day, and over every three to four years, the hair on our head is replaced.

The hair cycle has three main phases: **anagen, catagen** and **telogen**.

Anagen is the growth phase when hair grows one centimetre every month. With scalp hair, anagen lasts about three to four years. Each scalp hair will grow a centimetre per month for thirty-six to forty-eight months before it dies. If it's never cut, this hair will be between thirty-six and forty-eight centimetres long at the end of the growth cycle.

But on the eyebrows, anagen lasts only two to three months and so eyebrows only grow two to three centimetres long.

Catagen is the breaking-down phase that lasts only two weeks. During this time the hair strand dies and the lower two thirds of the hair follicle is completely destroyed. The hair remains in place during this period but does not continue to grow.

Telogen is the dormant phase of the hair cycle. It lasts around three months and for most of this phase the dead hair strand remains firmly anchored in the follicle until the new hair that's growing pushes it out. Shedding of the telogen hair is called **exogen** which can occur before or after the new anagen hair has started growing.

The hairs you notice coming out each day with brushing, combing, washing and shaking are telogen hairs. They've stopped growing, are dead and can be recognised by their white bulb at the root. Anagen hairs only come out when plucked. Ouch! You can tell them by their living, black and sticky bulbs that have a rich nerve supply.

On any given day between 50 and 150 dead telogen hairs will be pushed out by newly growing anagen hairs. If you look carefully, you will find them on your clothes, pillow case, hair brush or shower basin. Some women, especially those with long hair, are very aware of this hairy exodus, however many barely notice any loss.

THE LIVING TRUTH

At the end of the telogen phase, when the old hairs are replaced by new ones, stem cells regenerate the follicle's entire lower portion. These stem cells are in a compartment of the hair follicle known as the hair bulge. Not only can they regenerate the entire hair bulb at the base of the follicle, they can also regenerate oil glands and skin if required following injury. You can pluck your eyebrows for twenty years yet the persistent critters just keep growing back.

Every new hair bulb produces a new hair that pushes out the old one as it grows. In the bulb, each living cell divides into two. One cell stays put to divide another day, while the other is inserted from below into the growing new hair. As this cell matures, it produces the protein, keratin, the main component of hair. With the incorporation of more and more keratin, the tip of the new strand is pushed through the pore of the follicle, much like squeezing toothpaste out of its tube.

But if the bulb in the follicle functions abnormally, the production of the new strand is affected. The actual process of balding occurs in the bulb within the follicle — where you can't see it.

3
Genes and hormones

The natural colour and curliness, or otherwise, of your hair is a genetic lottery. So too is the matter of whether or not you are going to keep producing the hair on your head by natural means. Yes, you can blame your parents for FPHL — even if neither they nor your siblings show any sign of hair thinning.

Androgenetic alopecia is the medical name for the process that produces female pattern hair loss. Alopecia comes from the Greek *alopekia* which means loss of hair or baldness, and androgenetic means due to the effect of both androgens and genes.

Rather than there being a single gene behind

FPHL, scientists now believe that at least five genes are involved. How these genes combine determines whether you will develop FPHL, how fast the condition will progress and how much hair you will ultimately lose.

A useful way to think about the genetics of FPHL is as a card game, in this case, five-gene poker where higher cards (aces, kings, queens, jacks) represent the hair loss genes. Let's say your father has an ace, a king, a three, a four and a five and as a result has little or no hair loss. Your mother also has an ace, a king, a three, a four and a five and has little or no hair loss. When your parents deal you your genetic cards, it could be that you end up with two aces and two kings and a five, in which case, you'll lose hair. Meanwhile, your sister may be dealt only threes, fours and fives and your brother, a couple of fives, a three, one ace and one king. Both your sister and brother will keep their hair.

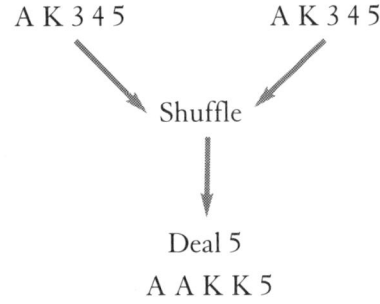

Of course if your father has four aces in his hand and went bald at twenty, and your mother was holding three aces and started losing hair at thirty-five, the deck is stacked against you and the chances of losing hair are high.

ANDROGENS

One thing we know for certain is that FPHL occurs when a woman with an inherited predisposition to the condition (i.e. they lost in the game of five-gene poker) is exposed to androgens.

Androgens are hormones that, amongst other things, affect cells in the hair follicle at a critical stage of hair growth. In women with a genetic predisposition to FPHL, androgens cause the *miniaturisation* of susceptible scalp hair follicles, that is, the affected follicles become smaller and smaller until they are no longer able to support normal hair production. Over time, this process results in affected scalp hairs becoming smaller, shorter and finer than the ones they are replacing. Hairs on the top of the head are more sensitive to androgens than those on the back of the head which in part explains the pattern of hair loss over the scalp.

WHERE DO ANDROGENS COME FROM?

Sex hormones are all produced from cholesterol. (Did you think cholesterol was bad for you?) In the ovaries, and also the adrenal glands that sit on top of your kidneys, cholesterol is converted into a range of hormones including oestrogen, progesterone and testosterone. Compared with men, women make only tiny amounts of testosterone, while men make only small amounts of oestrogen and progesterone.

Besides producing our hair and nails, skin has all the necessary equipment to convert cholesterol into sex hormones. It's some organ! On top of that, the ratio of the various sex hormones can be altered in the skin by local metabolism.

This means the androgens that drive hair loss can arrive either ready-made in the blood or be manufactured locally. And hormones that do arrive ready-made can be altered by the skin when they get there. Scalp skin responds to the hormones differently to armpit skin. In fact, different parts of the body alter the hormones differently. The net effect is that with puberty, hair grows in some places (armpits and pubic region), disappears in some places (FPHL), while other areas remain largely unchanged (eyebrows and eyelashes).

CONTRADICTION?

But don't androgens make hair grow? Yes, armpit and pubic hair growth at puberty is also caused by androgens, and this apparent paradox is a source of great confusion in the community.

Before puberty the follicles in our armpits and pubic areas produce short, fine, white hairs that are almost impossible to see. With the onset of puberty, androgen hormones stimulate these hair follicles making them larger and thus leading them to produce long, coarse, coloured hairs. This process occurs in stages. At first the hairs produced are only half a centimetre long, however, with each successive cycle the hairs grow progressively longer, coarser, thicker, darker and eventually curly as well. But remember, they have a limited shelf life and will rarely grow more than a few centimetres in length. FPHL is the reverse of this process and also occurs in stages. Early stages tend to go unnoticed, particularly in women who cut their hair short. But over time and after a number of successive hair cycles, their hair loss becomes apparent to them.

Scientists are starting to understand how the same hormones trigger different and opposite changes in hair growth on different parts of the body. Their research will hopefully lead to new and different treatments for both FPHL and unwanted body hair.

HORMONAL DISORDERS

Women with hormonal disorders such as polycystic ovarian syndrome, commonly develop FPHL. It may occur together with unwanted facial or body hair, irregular periods, low fertility and acne. When they're present together, these symptoms require further investigation by your doctor (blood tests and sometimes an ultrasound). Fortunately, hormone disorders are relatively uncommon. Fewer than ten per cent of women with scalp hair loss have a hormonal abnormality.

WHEN IT HAPPENED TO ME ...
Susanne, 32

Susanne started losing her hair about eighteen months ago. She noticed her hair was thinner than it used to be but it wasn't until excessive shedding occurred that she started to worry.

> Every time I went to a hairdresser or doctor they told me it was most likely due to stress and that I had plenty of hair. They made me feel I was complaining about nothing.

Her friends tried to be sympathetic by telling her that even if she was losing her hair, at least she didn't have a life-threatening disease, such as cancer. Susanne was grateful she didn't have cancer, but this did not help her deal with the problem.

Susanne's mother had thinning hair but it hadn't begun to show until she was in her fifties. Susanne had always imagined her mother's hair loss was due to wearing a nurses' cap and having too many perms.

'I was only thirty-two years old and all my friends had beautiful and healthy looking hair. Why was this happening to me?'

She decided to do her own research about thinning hair. On the Internet she discovered many women suffer from female pattern hair loss. And through the Internet she tracked down a dermatologist who specialised in hair loss diseases. A biopsy confirmed she did have FPHL, leaving her devastated.

'I cried for about two days straight.'

Like many other women diagnosed with female pattern hair loss, Susanne is struggling to come to terms with it. 'It's something I think about on a daily basis and I'm amazed at the impact this has on my life. The first thing I do when I meet a person is look at their hair. I try not to obsess but I have noticed there are many women who have it.'

Susanne has been on medical treatment (spironolactone) for six months but still has excessive hair shedding.

'I have to play the waiting game and keep taking the medication for at least twelve months in order to see improvement.'

Susanne now has a partner who is supporting her and sharing her life.

4
The impact of hair loss

Perhaps because FPHL is less socially obvious and neither expected nor understood by most women, it can be a frightening and confusing experience.

The main effect of FPHL is psychological. Apart from the dread of losing more hair, women begin to experience a range of changes related to guilt, medical treatment, body image, sleep and day-to-day functioning. Many women restrict their social activities because hair is very much a part of gender identity and attractiveness. They can feel ugly, masculinised and embarrassed. Some don't even want to leave the house.

Dutch, English and Australian studies of women seeking treatment for FPHL have found the condition is stressful and debilitating for the majority of sufferers. Three quarters have a lowered self-esteem and half have other social difficulties such as social anxiety, a negative body image, feelings of jealousy towards women who have thick hair, a sense of powerlessness to stop hair loss and frustration.

A woman's hair is a signal of her femininity, beauty and sexuality. Commonly women say, 'If my hair looks good, I look attractive no matter what I'm wearing, or how I look otherwise,' and, 'If my hair isn't right, nothing else can make me feel that I look good.'

And yet the degree to which hair loss affects women can differ greatly. The level of distress felt is not related to the severity of hair loss. For example, two women with different grades of hair loss may both feel the same level of distress, while a third woman who has a higher grade loss may be much more comfortable with her condition.

FIRST REACTIONS

When women are diagnosed with female pattern hair loss after all other explanations have been eliminated, they usually experience shock. Some women report having been so stunned they didn't hear another thing their doctor said afterwards. Most admit to going home and crying, sometimes for days.

For many women the shock is followed by intense sadness and helplessness at having a life-long, appearance-altering condition. Some feel their identity is being stripped away from them all of a sudden and there's nothing they can do about it. This sadness may last for some time, and two years after being diagnosed, women often say they are still coming to terms with the news.

Because female pattern hair loss is not well known or well understood by the general public, newly diagnosed women can feel very alone and isolated. They may feel there is no one they can talk to about how they're feeling, or that no one will be able to understand. It's important, at this early stage, that they contact their local alopecia support group (see p. 147) and consider seeking counselling. They are usually surprised to find how many others are affected by the condition and discover that sharing experiences is very helpful.

Now is a good time for a woman to confide in a

trusted friend or family member about her condition. The first few months after diagnosis can be particularly difficult and having someone close and supportive can help ease the way. It may be useful to think about the period between receiving the diagnosis and successfully adjusting to the condition as a period of mourning. Newly diagnosed women need time to grieve for the loss of their former alopecia-free life, before they can be expected to embrace the challenges of their new life.

KEEPING IT UNDER YOUR HAT

A lot of women struggle with the dilemma of going public with their hair loss or 'keeping it under their hat'. There are pros and cons to each approach which need to be weighed up by each individual.

Many choose to conceal it from all but their closest friends and family. They don't want people who didn't know them pre-alopecia to make judgements about them based on their diagnosis. Quite reasonably, they don't want to be identified with their condition.

Other women choose to conceal their condition

in the interest of others. For example, a mother with female pattern hair loss may choose not to tell her young daughter so that the girl doesn't grow up worrying about whether she has inherited it. That bridge can be crossed if and when it is encountered.

Another compelling reason for keeping your hair loss condition to yourself is to avoid unpleasant and sometimes strange reactions from others. These come from all kinds of people — kids, adults, even hair and health professionals. Children tend to call it as they see it: 'Mummy, why has that lady got no hair?' 'Daddy, I can see that lady's skull!' But the most common negative reaction from adults is dismissal: 'What are you talking about? You've got loads of hair.' 'You're imagining things.' 'Women don't go bald, silly!' 'It could be worse …' Or, 'You know, your problem is you're too stressed. You just need to relax and then it'll grow back.'

In addition to the physical effects, women frequently feel as though they need to conceal the emotional effects of hair loss. They don't want to appear vain or obsessed with their appearance, nor do they want to come across as someone whose life is ruled by it. They want to be seen as the confident, capable and attractive woman they know they are, despite their thinning hair. They don't want to be perceived as sad, anxious women with poor self esteem. So, even though they might put on a brave face, the woman with hair loss is often struggling with thoughts and feelings that seriously impact upon her day-to-day life.

For some women, going public is an important stage in accepting their hair loss. Letting people know that you have the condition also means acknowledging the role the condition plays in your life. In fact, for some women, going public can be a huge relief as it involves saving all the energy spent each day trying to conceal the problem.

GUILT

A surprising reaction for many women is their strong feeling of guilt: guilt over caring so much about their appearance and guilt for feeling so bad about their hair loss. Powerful personal and social factors contribute to these feelings. Perhaps the strongest are the Western beliefs that: 1) vanity is bad, and 2) there is always someone worse off than you.

THE IMPACT OF HAIR LOSS

Most of us would agree that a person's worth does not depend on their physical beauty, but on who they are on the inside. Yet the media tells us a different story. We are bombarded with images of stars with fabulous, thick flowing hair. Lots of hair means health, success, glamour, style. In fact, it seems that all the money, success and fame in the world isn't enough unless it's topped off by a good head of hair. Just ask Donald Trump.

This situation leads to a troubling circle of thoughts for women with hair loss. It goes something like this:

> Beauty is only skin deep. I don't judge my friends and family on their appearance, so why would people judge me on mine? And I know that I'm an attractive and valuable person on the inside. So why do I feel so awful? Because people see me as a thin-haired person. That's not who I am! It makes me angry that people can't see who I really am. But is my identity completely tied up in my appearance? Am I really that vain? Of course not! So why do I care? Oh, I'm such a hypocrite! I should feel okay about my hair loss. It's just my hair, after all. I could always

> wear a hat, or a wig, or … but that's not me! I don't want people to think I'm a wig-wearing weirdo! But why should I care? If I was having chemotherapy, I wouldn't think twice about wearing a scarf or a hat. But that would be a temporary situation — I would eventually go back to being me. I'm such a vain hypocrite!

Another version of hair loss–related guilt takes a slightly different form but ends up at the same place. It's the 'feeling bad for feeling bad' version and goes something like this:

> I hate this condition; it's so depressing. But, hey, at least I'm healthy, have a good job, good friends, a loving partner. I really shouldn't feel so bad. But I *do*. I cried for weeks when I was diagnosed and it's the first thing I think of every morning when I wake up. There are people suffering all over the world and in my own community. People who are really sick, or don't have all the great things in their lives that I have. I really don't deserve to feel bad. I'm so shallow! I didn't realise how shallow and how selfish I am until now. Am I really that

pathetic? But I *hate* it! Why me? Why do I have to be punished like this? I'd rather have just about any other disease than this. Oh, that's a terrible thing to think! I can't believe I even thought it! I am *so* self-centred. I have no right to feel bad. At least I'm healthy and have a roof over my head. So why do I think about my hair every minute of the day?

The end point of both trains of thought is feeling like a bad person. But that needn't be the case. Both versions are perfectly normal responses to appearance-altering medical conditions in Western cultures. In these cultures, hair *is* important in the sense that it reflects an individual's attitudes, beliefs and values and is a way of communicating to others who we are. We use our hair to tell the world what kind of music we like (think of rockers with their quiffs), the kind of lifestyle we adopt (the hippy's natural locks, untouched by product), or the type of job we do (the clipped head of a soldier). So it's okay to experience these feelings of guilt but, as we all know, nothing comes of feeling guilty. It won't change society, it won't make hair thicker and, well, it feels bad!

IF ONLY I HAD MY HAIR, I'D BE HAPPY

If you suffer from female pattern hair loss, you've probably thought, my life would be perfect, if only I had my hair back. You might feel as though the return of a full head of hair would wash away any negatives in your life.

That's a lot of pressure to put on your hair! Its loss can make you feel as though your health and happiness is riding on your hair-do. As though you're having just one big bad hair day.

IT'S ALL I THINK ABOUT!

FPHL can be an extremely distressing, not to mention exhausting condition. For many women, the first thing they think in the morning is, 'How much hair am I going to lose today?' It's on their mind all day long as they attempt to conceal their condition, wonder if anyone has noticed it and worry about it getting worse. Women can come to dread showering and styling their hair each morning and seeing their hair go down the drain or come away in their brush.

If you find yourself thinking about your hair all

day, you're not being over-sensitive or vain, and you're not alone. Even women with full heads of hair spend a fair amount of time and effort each day thinking about their hair's appearance and trying to keep it under some kind of control, so why shouldn't you?

It becomes a problem when your thoughts about your hair begin to impact on your wellbeing and daily life. Some women cover all the mirrors in their home so they can avoid seeing their own reflection and reminding themselves of their hair loss. Others stay toward the rear when walking down the street with a group so their companions won't see the back of their head. Some arrive early to work and social functions so that they can secure the seat in the darkest corner of the room.

Being constantly and acutely aware of your hair has other, flow-on psychological effects. You may begin to imagine that, like you, everyone else is always thinking about your hair and you may become a vigilant hair monitor yourself.

Because you spend so much time thinking about and monitoring your hair, it may feel as though people are staring at your hair, talking about your hair, or judging you because of your hair. In short, you start to get a bit paranoid about the whole thing. Again, this is a perfectly normal response to an appearance-altering condition. It's the same when you develop a pimple on your nose. You know it's red, it feels large and noticeable, and you think everyone is staring at it and disgusted by it. Chances are other people don't spend as much time thinking about your hair as you think they do. Sure, they may notice your condition, but do they really discuss it around the water cooler? Do *you* talk about your colleague's acne around the water cooler?

The other effect of focusing on your hair loss is that you start monitoring other people's hair. You check out the hair of every woman you meet, assess whether they have female pattern hair loss and whether it is more or less severe than your own. A similar thing happens when you buy a new car. You don't notice how many of your model are on the road until you have one yourself — then you see your car everywhere! Similarly, many women are amazed at how common female pattern hair loss is in the general population.

You may even use other women's hair loss conditions as a benchmark for your own. Based on another woman's age and stage of hair loss, you calculate the future progression of your own hair loss. Of course, this rather unscientific approach can be comfort or a nightmare, depending on whether the woman you have picked as your benchmark has retained or lost most of her hair. Either way, it's best to avoid comparing your hair with others' as the course of the condition is different for every woman.

Even though they may seem a little irrational, the thoughts and feelings described here are real and can leave you feeling upset, depressed and exhausted.

In the next chapter we'll look at ways of keeping your feelings under control.

WHEN IT HAPPENED TO ME ...
Marie, 62

'Hello! I'm a person! Look down at my eyes and not my head.'

Marie was devastated and depressed when she first started to lose her hair. What made it worse was her friends' lack of understanding. Some would say to her, 'Hair loss! That's nonsense! You've always had thin hair.' She would prefer people to acknowledge she has alopecia.

> I can't help feeling a little distressed if a friend denies I have alopecia. I also get upset when people tell me stories about people they know whose hair fell out and grew back again. They obviously don't understand female pattern hair loss is different from, say, hair loss caused by a traumatic event.

How did Marie become strong?

> It crept up on me very gradually. I think it's from being aware of the world around you and how it all works. I discovered people actually don't care if you've got hair or not. They care about who you are, if you are a good person and if you're fun to be with. I also have friends who have physical disabilities and they get on with their lives. They don't allow their disabilities to hold them back. So I think I get strength from other people and seeing how they cope with difficulties in their lives. What helps is using common

sense, a good sense of humour, and support from family and friends. Initially, when I shared my problem with people they would have a conversation with me staring at the top of my head which is very disconcerting.

For Marie, coping with her thinning hair is something she needs to work at. She still has her bad days but finds the courage to get on with her life. She tries to avoid looking at her hair in the mirror, especially looking at the back of her head — 'That's not a good idea!' Staff meetings at work were a nuisance — she used to sit in the back row so people wouldn't see the balding area at the back of her head. She now feels comfortable sitting up the front.

'I decided my hair wasn't going to dictate how I should live my life!'

5
Thoughts, feelings and coping

It can be difficult to deal with the troubling thoughts, beliefs and behaviours related to your hair loss if you haven't developed the skills to calm yourself physically and mentally.

Anxiety is a perfectly natural and important response to events that threaten our wellbeing, safety, or even life. It's our body saying, 'I don't like it. What are we going to do about it? I'm ready for action!' A little bit of anxiety plays an important and positive role in everyday situations. It gets us into action when we're running late for an appointment, it gets our blood pumping before a date, it ensures we study before an exam. So, a bit of anxiety in the right amounts and at the right time is a good thing. But when it rules your day it's got out of hand.

Thinking about the purpose of anxiety reactions can help you understand how your own anxiety about your hair loss impacts on your life. The anxiety response developed millions of years ago, when we walked the tundra where sabre-toothed tigers hid behind every tree. If one were to jump in front of you, it would be fatal to just stand there, casually brushing the dust off your clothes. Fortunately, humans evolved the anxiety response which prepares our bodies either to stay and fight, or run for our life — the 'fight or flight' response. It doesn't occur just in the mind, it's a full-body affair.

When we encounter danger, an array of things happens. Unnecessary physical functions such as digestion slow down or stop, and physical resources are redirected toward vital functions that will keep you alive. Here is what you could expect to experience when encountering a tiger in the wild:

- ✂ Airways open up (open mouth, flared nostrils)
- ✂ Breathing becomes more rapid
- ✂ Mental activity increases

THOUGHTS, FEELINGS AND COPING

- Blood vessels constrict
- Heart beats faster
- Blood pressure rises
- Blood flow to skin decreases
- Digestion shuts down
- Mouth becomes dry
- Glucose is mobilised
- Muscle strength increased
- Pupils dilate
- Sweating increases
- Kidneys decrease output
- Bowel and bladder sphincters close
- Immune system is suppressed

The net effect of this response is that you're ready for action. So anxiety when you are about to be attacked by a tiger is good! However, you might recognise some of the physical effects listed above from your day-to-day, tiger-free life. Perhaps you are meeting friends after work for a drink at the local wine bar and your palms start to sweat, your breathing becomes quick and shallow. You might even feel nauseous. If this is the case, you're having a tiger-level response to a wine-bar-level event. Or, more relevantly, to a *hair loss* event.

Tiger-level anxiety responses are rarely

required in most women's daily life. When they occur in the absence of a tiger, they can severely impair your functioning and prevent you doing the things you want to do and being the person you know you are.

Dealing with anxiety is a two-stage process.

The **first stage** involves learning to relax your body and mind.

The **second stage** involves addressing the thoughts, feeling and behaviours that cause your tiger-level anxiety.

We recommend you spend at least one week developing your relaxation skills before tackling thoughts, beliefs and behaviours.

RELAXATION

Relaxing is *not* the same as napping ... it's something you do when you are fully conscious. It involves thoughts and behaviours that are consciously produced with the sole purpose of reducing physical and psychological anxiety. So, no relaxing at bedtime!

Before starting your relaxation techniques, you might want to consider reducing your intake of caffeine (coffee, cola and energy drinks), refined sugars (lollies, cakes and takeaway food), alcohol and nicotine. Despite what the advertisements say, these products won't relax you. It might feel as though they do, but the pleasurable sensations associated with them probably have more to do with satisfaction of cravings (nicotine), the associated burst of energy (caffeine and sugar), or the reduction of inhibitions (alcohol). When it comes to relaxation, these products, in fact, inhibit your natural self-soothing mechanisms.

Progressive muscle relaxation and **controlled breathing** are two popular and effective relaxation techniques. Both produce the relaxation response where:

- Our muscles relax and we behave in a relaxed way
- Our blood pressure and heart rate decreases
- We produce fewer stress hormones
- The oxygen and carbon dioxide content of our blood becomes balanced
- Our immune system functions better
- Our energy is increased

Progressive muscle relaxation is a technique for producing deep and long-lasting relaxation and takes fifteen to twenty minutes. This technique is most effective when practised in a quiet, comfortable location where you won't be interrupted.

Controlled breathing can help you to reduce anxiety on the run quickly, any place, any time. It's useful just before you walk into a meeting, get up to make a presentation, or prepare for a night out. No one will know you are doing it and it takes only about thirty seconds.

You'll find helpful instructions on relaxation techniques and controlled breathing in the Appendix on page 135.

MANAGING YOUR THOUGHTS AND FEELINGS

The diagram on the facing page shows how anxiety can work for us or against us. You can see as your level of anxiety initially increases, so does your performance or proficiency. But as your anxiety further increases, performance becomes worse.

Imagine you're going for your driver's licence tomorrow. If you're not at all anxious about it, you may not have bothered to study the road rules very closely. You may have decided you don't really need a last-minute lesson and, on the day, not really care whether you pass or not. If you're as relaxed as this, you'll probably fail.

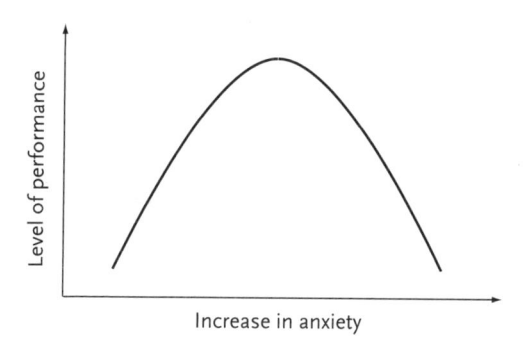

[Graph: Level of performance (y-axis) vs Increase in anxiety (x-axis), showing an inverted U-shaped curve]

On the other hand, if you are highly anxious about the test, you might stay up all night poring over your book of road rules and plan a three-hour last-minute lesson just before your test. You might be so anxious that you can't even eat breakfast. Obviously, in this frenzied, tired and hungry state, you're not going to perform to the best of your ability. You might find you overreact to traffic, or become so confused you forget how to parallel park.

Ideally, you want to be somewhere in between: anxious enough to care about how you perform, and alert to the challenges of the situation, but relaxed enough to sleep the night before and, on the day, able to concentrate on the job that needs to be done.

The aim here is not to help you to eliminate *all* anxiety and stress from your life. Rather, it's to help you to sort out the good from the bad feelings, the reasonable from the unreasonable thoughts, and the helpful from the unhelpful behaviours. The goal is to reach a balance that allows you to live the kind of life you want to live.

COGNITIVE-BEHAVIOURAL TECHNIQUES

Cognitive-behavioural techniques for managing thoughts, feelings and behaviours are based on the assumption that the three are interrelated. That is, your feelings can affect your behaviour, your behaviour can affect your thoughts and your thoughts can affect your feelings. Take the following scenario.

Emma has Grade 3 female pattern hair loss. She's having a particularly ghastly hair day and this morning she can't make her hair do anything. The more she tries to style it (behaviour), the more frustrated she becomes (feeling). Eventually, she has to leave the house and go to work.

She drives along the road and at every set of lights plays with her hair, trying to coax it into order (behaviour). She thinks she looks ugly (thought) and feels helpless (feeling) because she knows she's not really ugly but her hair is letting her down. As she pulls into her workplace, she sees a couple of colleagues. They're looking her way and laughing.

Emma thinks they're laughing at her hair (thought). She's angry and embarrassed (feeling) and walks through the door thoroughly miserable (feeling). She thinks everybody can tell and is watching her (thought) as she heads for her office. Later that morning she cancels the dinner she had planned with friends for that night (behaviour).

Let's look at how Emma's thoughts, feelings and behaviours feed each other, and consider some techniques for stopping the cycle. By changing one element, we can change the others.

Thinking about feeling

If someone asks you why you are so happy today,

you might answer, 'because my football team made the finals,' or, 'because I had a great day at work,' or, 'because I'm having dinner with my friends tonight.'

Some event has caused your happiness. An *activating event* has caused certain *consequences*.

Likewise, when you're feeling sad you might say that it's, 'because I broke up with my partner,' or, 'because I hate my job,' or, 'because I never have any money.' Once again, you can identify activating events that appear to cause certain emotional consequences.

This way of thinking about feelings is called A → C thinking. A is the **A**ctivating event and C is the emotional or behavioural **C**onsequences. We have a tendency to accept that A causes C: slow drivers make me angry; a new leather jacket will make me feel better; I'm unlovable because I'm overweight; my boss forced me to resign.

Now, if A → C thinking is correct, everyone experiencing the same event should experience the same consequences. For example, three friends visiting the National Gallery of Australia stand in front of Jackson Pollock's *Blue Poles*. Ann says the painting makes her feel a bit sad; Jill has no

THOUGHTS, FEELINGS AND COPING

feelings about the painting and moves on; Joan says the painting makes her feel angry.

How can the same activating event — viewing a painting — produce such varied emotional consequences (sadness, indifference and anger)? There must be something an individual brings to the situation that produces a particular emotional or behavioural consequence for them. Enter the Bs.

B stands for your **B**eliefs and attitudes and it's these Beliefs and attitudes, not the Activating event, which really cause the Cs. A → B → C thinking goes like this:

> **A** is the event that activates **B**
>
> **B** is your beliefs and attitudes which lead to **C**
>
> **C** are the consequences

Returning to Ann, Jill and Joan. What might be the **B**eliefs that *Blue Poles* **A**ctivates causing the emotional **C**onsequences of sadness, indifference and anger? Conversations with each of the women might go something like this:

> YOU: Ann, why does the painting make you feel sad?

ANN: Well, it's not the painting so much as the artist. Pollock had such a troubled life, what with the alcoholism and all. I look at this painting and I feel sad for the genius who died in his prime. It's just so unfair.

This painting has **A**ctivated specific **B**eliefs Ann has about Pollock being a tortured genius who suffered for his art and was lost to the world before his time.

Let's move on to Jill.

YOU: Jill, the painting didn't seem to have much effect on you. Why?

JILL: I don't know. I just don't like the colours, I suppose.

It's fair to say that the painting didn't **A**ctivate any of Jill's **B**eliefs or attitudes, except perhaps her attitude to the colour blue.

And finally, Joan.

YOU: Joan, why does the painting make you angry?

JOAN: Because it's ridiculous and meaningless!

YOU: How so?

JOAN: Well, because the artist was a drunk and

had no real skill apart from throwing around tins of paint.

YOU: Would it make a difference if the artist was sober and an excellent draughtsman?

JOAN: No! It's still rubbish. I can't believe that's what they spend our tax dollars on!

YOU: So you're annoyed your tax dollar is being spent on bad art?

JOAN: Huh! I wouldn't even call it art! It's just a ... just a ... a mess!

In this brief discussion we get closer to the **B**elief causing Joan's anger. Perhaps it's a **B**elief that art produced by sober, clean-living artists is the only good art. Perhaps it's a **B**elief that she should be able to understand art and that this splattered mess confuses her and makes her feel unsure about herself. Perhaps Joan holds the **B**elief that abstract art is a waste of time and money. If we dig a little deeper, we may even uncover the deeper **B**eliefs that cause the surface beliefs. Why *does* Joan have such strong feelings about drunken artists? Were her own artistic efforts criticised by someone she respected?

As you can see, investigating **B**eliefs can be an unsettling job!

The consequence of adopting B → C thinking is that you are required to take responsibility for your own feelings, thoughts and behaviours. Confronting your **B**eliefs and attitudes and accepting responsibility for your thoughts, feelings and behaviours can itself be anxiety-provoking. This is why your relaxation strategies are so important. They'll help you keep a handle on your anxiety levels, making it easier for you to think clearly and rationally about your situation.

CHALLENGING UNHELPFUL BELIEFS

We've seen how an individual's **B**eliefs cause particular emotional and behavioural **C**onsequences, but how do you manage unhelpful beliefs? Let's go back to Emma who has Grade 3 hair loss and who is having a bad start to her day.

As she pulls into her work place, she sees a couple of colleagues. They're looking her way and laughing. She thinks they're laughing at her hair. She feels angry and embarrassed and walks through the door feeling thoroughly miserable.

The **A**ctivating event here is seeing her colleagues looking in her direction and laughing. The **C**onsequences are that she feels angry, embarrassed and miserable. The **B**elief causing the **C**onsequences is that her colleagues are laughing at her because of her hair loss. But is Emma justified in believing this? Are her colleagues really laughing at her? Are they really that mean, and is she justified in being so upset? Is there another explanation for their laughing?

Once you've identified the **B**eliefs causing the emotional consequences, you need to look closely at them and decide whether they are well founded. You can do this by asking yourself the following questions:

> Is there any objective evidence that my **B**elief is correct?
>
> If my **B**elief *is* correct, what's the worst thing about it? Is it so bad I can't handle it?

Thinking about Emma's **B**elief that her colleagues are laughing at her hair, do you think she's justified in her **B**elief? A conversation with Emma might go something like this:

You: Emma, why are you so upset?

Emma: I caught Bob and Julie laughing at my thinning hair.

You: You did? How rude! What did they say?

Emma: I don't know, I just saw them laughing.

You: At you … ?

Emma: Yeah, I was pulling in to the car park and they were coming out the door and looking right at me and laughing.

You: Oh, I don't think they were actually laughing at you.

Emma: But they were looking right at me.

You: Well, maybe, but just before Bob and Julie went outside, Kim told a really funny story about his dog eating the leg of lamb he was cooking for his in-laws. Everyone was laughing their heads off.

Emma: Oh.

We always have to entertain the possibility that our beliefs are wrong and the only way to check that out is to ask ourselves, 'Where's the evidence?'

Unless you genuinely seek evidence for your Belief, you're not really justified in clinging to it.

And it's not really fair on other people involved — in Emma's case, Bob and Julie. Another way of checking whether your **B**eliefs are correct, or at least reasonable, is to ask yourself, 'Can I think of another explanation for the event?' As we saw, the real explanation for Bob and Julie's laughter may have had nothing at all to do with Emma.

But what if Emma had been right and Bob and Julie *were* laughing at her? Sometimes, when we check out the **B**eliefs that lead to emotional **C**onsequences, we find they are, in fact, correct. What do you do then? Let's go back to Emma.

YOU: Emma, why are you so upset?

EMMA: I caught Bob and Julie laughing at my thinning hair.

YOU: I actually heard them joking about your hair just before they went outside. Not very subtle, are they?

EMMA: You can say that again. I'm so embarrassed. I don't feel like I can even leave my office.

YOU: Why?

EMMA: Because they'll laugh at me again.

YOU: So?

Emma: It's awful! And embarrassing! *You* wouldn't want to be laughed at.

You: No, you're right there. I hate being laughed at, but I suppose I can't stop people laughing at whatever they want to.

Emma: I suppose.

You: Anyway, do you really care what they think? Do they really have that sort of power over you?

Emma: No, don't be silly.

You: But you say they can keep you from coming out of your office. I wish I had that sort of power over my boss!

Emma: Of course they don't have power over me. But everyone in the office will know about it. I'll be the laughing stock.

You: Know about what? Your hair loss problem?

Emma: Yes!

You: Emma, everyone in the office already knows about your condition.

Emma: But ... how?

You: They're not blind! They've known for months!

Emma: But no one has said anything.

You: Why would they? Sorry Emma, you're just not that fascinating! We do have more interesting things to talk about, you know ... like the new guy over in despatch.

Emma: Hmmm, good point.

If, like Emma, you find that the **B**eliefs causing your upsetting emotions are true, you need to decide how big a deal it is.

Ask yourself, 'Do I really care if some people laugh at me? Everybody is laughed at some time or another. It's not as if I have a card that gives me diplomatic immunity from being laughed at just because I have female pattern hair loss. Nope, everyone is fair game, I suppose. Doesn't mean I have to like it, but since there's nothing I can do about other people's laughing habits, why waste my time and energy worrying about it? Sometimes it's going to hurt, but I can handle it.'

So where did Emma's **B**elief come from? Remember, she had just spent the morning desperately trying to style her hair to cover her thinning scalp. If she is so aware of her scalp, she imagines everyone else must be, too. And they must hate it as much as she does, and think she's ugly like she does, and so on. Sometimes **B**eliefs can develop a life of their own!

If we look a little closer, we can uncover an even deeper **B**elief. If Bob and Julie really were laughing at Emma's hair loss, so what? Why should Emma care? Because she holds the **B**elief that laughing at people is mean and cruel and that she shouldn't be laughed at because it's not her fault she has female pattern hair loss.

Is this reasonable? Why should Emma be the only person in the world that shouldn't be laughed at? Why is she so special? Everyone gets embarrassed, angry and sad at some time or another — it's part of being human. And some people are mean and cruel and laugh at others' misfortunes. But is Emma really going to change them? Probably not. Anyway, she's got more important things to spend her time and energy on ... like that guy in despatch.

To summarise, you can change the way you think and, consequently, the way you feel, by doing the following:

- Identify your **A**, **B** and **C**
- Evaluate the **B** for accuracy
  - Do you have any objective evidence?
  - Have you genuinely tried to find out if it's true or not?
  - Have you tested your beliefs to see if they hold?
- If your **B**s turn out to be accurate, work on dealing with the **C**s they cause
- If your **B**s turn out to be irrational, develop some rational alternative **B**s.

THOUGHT STOPPING AND SCHEDULED WORRYING

Many women with female pattern hair loss find they think about their condition all day, every day. In particular, they worry about their condition getting worse; what they can do to prevent further hair loss; what other people think of them; and what the future holds. This can be exhausting and take up a lot of time that could be better spent on more pleasant activities.

We all know worrying about something will not stop it occurring, yet sometimes we feel we have to worry about things, otherwise something bad will happen. We need to hang on to the thought or feeling to stop it getting out of our control. And the more we worry about it, the more we feel we need to worry about it. When you find yourself stuck in a worry loop like this, ask yourself the following questions:

- Do I have any evidence that worrying about this will help?
- Am I trying to control things I can't possibly control?
- Will this even matter to me next year, next month or next week?
- When I'm on my deathbed, will I regret not having worried more about this?

If the answers to these questions don't interrupt your worry loop, you might want to try **thought stopping** or **scheduled worrying**.

Thought stopping involves catching yourself in a worry loop and stopping it. This requires a bit of practice, but it gradually becomes easier and more effective. Initially, this technique requires a timer, whether it's an egg timer, the timer on the microwave or the stopwatch function on your mobile phone.

Set your timer for sixty seconds and concentrate on the worrisome problem as intently as you can. When the sixty seconds are up, say to yourself, 'Stop!' and force the thought out of your mind. You might even punctuate this by pinching the back of your hand or even saying 'Stop!' out loud. After a while you won't need to wait sixty seconds to escape the worry loop — you'll recognise the worrisome thoughts as they appear and send them away at your will.

Scheduled worrying involves setting aside twenty minutes a day, dedicated solely to worrying about things. In this way, you do the worrying you want to do, but it doesn't interfere with your daily activity. It works like this.

Throughout the day, as worrying thoughts enter your mind and threaten to take over, jot them down in a notebook and put it aside to be worried about later. It's best to schedule your worrying for the afternoon or evening when you have gathered a full day's worth of things to worry about. If you think you have too many things to be adequately worried about in twenty minutes, you can carry some over to the next day's session. In time, you'll find worrisome thoughts invade your mind less and less often as they no longer get the attention they used to.

THE CHALLENGES OF CHANGE

Change is anxiety provoking — even good change! It's worthwhile noting that in the rankings of stressful life events, getting married ranks seventh, ahead of getting the sack and the death of a close friend. So change of any kind is challenging and requires energy and adjustment.

Adjusting to a diagnosis of female pattern hair loss is particularly challenging and you can expect to have good days, bad days and really bad days. Tackling the negative thoughts, feelings and behaviours associated with your condition can be a tough job. You will have to look closely at some of your most fundamental beliefs and attitudes. Sometimes you'll pleasantly surprise yourself, but in others you might not like what you find.

It's important to remember your relaxation techniques (Appendix, p. 135) as you look at the beliefs and attitudes that underlie your thoughts, behaviours and feelings. This is not always a pleasant experience so be prepared to manage the anxiety that's bound to arise. If you find it difficult to tackle all this you can contact a counsellor or psychologist who offers cognitive behavioural therapy (see Useful Resources, p. 147).

WHEN IT HAPPENED TO ME ...
Julie, 38

Being a woman with hair loss has affected Julie's life in so many ways she believes she's a completely different person to whom she might have been, had this not happened to her. She was twenty-six and starting to feel confident and happy with herself when she first noticed her hair thinning.

'I'm sure that I don't even realise all the ways that I've changed, but what I do know is that my confidence and self-esteem has all but gone.'

Julie's mood is completely dependent on how she is feeling about her hair, and catching sight of it in a changing room mirror can be enough to send her home crying.

Avoidance strategies have become second nature to her. She doesn't bend down to pick up an object or stand in line where people could look closely at the top of her head. She'll arrive early at a restaurant so she can choose the seat with the least overhead lighting, and she always sits in the back row of a lecture or meeting. She doesn't go swimming and doesn't venture out when it's windy or raining. She spends a lot of energy trying to keep what's left of her hair from being blown all over the place.

Julie finds visits to the hairdresser are difficult.

'Everyone's hair is beautiful when you have next to none of your own.'

Spending a couple of hours focusing solely on her hair is not pleasant, particularly when surrounded by women with plenty of hair. Julie believes she would be a 'nicer' person if it weren't for her hair, but instead she is depressed most of the time.

> I know it's not true, but I often think that my life could be perfect and I could cope with anything if I didn't have to worry about my hair.

At a visit to her doctor Julie picked up a flyer that offered a psychological group program for women with hair loss — the Halo Program (see p. 153). Three months passed before she phoned.

> I wasn't sure at first about participating, but after speaking to the facilitator who was sympathetic I was glad I did. It was great to meet and listen to other women talk about their hair loss experiences, and to know there are others struggling emotionally with this condition.

6
Styling, camouflaging and replacing

I've come to the conclusion I need a hair cut! It hasn't been cut for about five years because my hair loss has become progressively worse. I'm embarrassed about how thin it is and I'm frightened of how the hairdresser will react. I need some help with styling so that I can disguise the thin top and sides. How do you cut and style it so that it hides my severe hair loss problem? This situation is very distressing and painful for me. I'm a single thirty-seven-year-old woman who used to have thick, flowing, curly locks.

— Sarah

Hair styling techniques, camouflage products, hair pieces and wigs will help you manage the day-to-day styling problems associated with hair loss. Finding the one that best suits your personality and lifestyle will improve your confidence and lessen the impact of your condition.

HAIR STYLING

A change of hairstyle can give you an immediate boost while you are exploring treatment options for your hair loss, and a well-selected style and colour can improve the appearance of your hair by making it appear thicker and fuller. Most women with female pattern hair loss dread going to the hairdresser. Some avoid it altogether because they're embarrassed about their hair. They feel uncomfortable sitting among women who don't have hair loss problems and frequently feel disappointed and upset with the hair cut they receive.

> I told my hairdresser I have thin hair and would like a style that will make it appear fuller. She responded by chopping and layering to make my hair appear fuller. Instead, it appeared even thinner and

> lacked buoyancy. I was devastated and left the salon in tears.
>
> — Jennifer

If you are unhappy with your hairstyle and need some advice on how to disguise your hair loss, you should seek a hairdresser with whom you'll feel comfortable discussing it. More importantly, you need to find a professional who has a complete understanding of this problem, and who is experienced in assisting affected women to find solutions that meet their physical and emotional needs. You may have to shop around and endure a few disappointments until you find a stylist you are satisfied with. But once you do, spread the word to others.

HOW DO I FIND THE BEST HAIRSTYLE FOR ME?

The most important factor for a woman with thinning hair is the style.

Hair needs to be properly cut and shaped to accentuate your best facial features, complement your lifestyle and, of course, minimise the appearance of your hair loss.

At your next appointment with the hairdresser you may want to ask for some suggestions on different styles and hairstyling tips that will improve your appearance and help you feel better about yourself. This may involve a completely different look and three or four haircuts before you find your optimal colour and look.

Thinning hair should be managed in a way that will give you back your lifestyle, so that you are not consistently on edge or anxious that your hair will move and reveal the thinning areas. Your hair loss should not inhibit you from doing things you enjoy such as swimming, dancing, or dating because there *are* solutions to your hairstyling challenges.

SUGGESTIONS FROM A PROFESSIONAL STYLIST

- ✂ Shorter styles will give you greater volume and lift.
- ✂ A side or zigzag parting, rather than central parting, will disguise the thinness at the top.
- ✂ Longer hair should be kept at a length that allows you to lift it in a chignon or a twist.
- ✂ Adding some soft layers on the top will give

STYLING, CAMOUFLAGING AND REPLACING

hair that is pulled back more style and takes some weight off the top.
- ✂ Comb wet hair using soft, wide-tooth combs or brushes designed to flow through your thin hair without breaking it.
- ✂ Towel-drying can damage thin hair. Instead, use a friction-free towel that blots hair and absorbs most of the moisture.
- ✂ Any colour can make hair look thicker and appear to give it more volume.
- ✂ A body wave with soft or tight curls can also give your hair more bounce and fullness.
- ✂ Use products labelled specifically for thinning hair. Styling sprays and volumising foams that have a lightweight formula create long-lasting hairstyles full of volume and movement. Hair spray can help set a style, but use formulas that are light and non-drying to prevent breakage.

HAIR CARE FALLACIES

- ✂ Lots of layers will give your thin hair more body — False! Layering actually thins out the hair and takes the bulk out of it.

- ✂ Blow-drying can damage thin hair — False! Heat from a blow-dryer won't actually damage your hair. Blow-drying incorrectly, however, can damage your hair by creating static and breakage.
- ✂ Conditioning thin hair will make it appear limp — False! A heavy conditioner that's not made specifically for thin hair can weigh your hair down. Instead, a lightweight conditioner is recommended.

CAMOUFLAGE

Camouflaging products, such as spray-on colour, creams and powders cover exposed areas on the scalp and hide the fact that you have hair loss. They can also provide lift at the base of the hair shaft, adding fullness. These products tend to best suit women who have mild to moderate hair loss while those who have lost more hair may not achieve a natural appearance after application. If used properly, people won't know you have thinning hair and you'll feel better about your appearance, less self-conscious and more confident.

Most camouflaging products are specially

formulated to not rub off easily, so you can exercise, perspire, or even go swimming without worrying about the product washing away or running down your face. To remove the camouflage, simply shampoo as usual. Best of all, camouflage products are compatible with topical minoxidil treatment.

Hair building fibres

These are keratin fibres (the same material your hair is made of) available in a range of natural hair colours from pale blonde through to black. They come in a jar with a pepper shaker-type top. Shaking the fibres lightly onto the thinning areas of your scalp creates density throughout the area and significantly reduces the appearance of thinning hair — a transformation that takes place in thirty seconds or less.

They do come in a range of colours, but if you have difficulty matching your own hair colour you can mix colours together to achieve the required shade.

Scalp spray thickeners

These are sprays that cover thinning areas by bonding fibres to your hair to create density and add colour. Several brands are available in various tints.

Unlike some of the other products, scalp spray thickeners can be a little messy to use, so take care to avoid getting the spray on your clothes and fingers when spraying your hair.

Alopecia masking lotion

This is a tinted lotion that is dabbed onto thinning areas of the scalp to create the illusion of fuller hair. It comes in a tube with a special applicator to help give your frontal hairline a fuller, yet natural, look. The lotion is not sticky or greasy and will not rub off or stain your clothing. One tube of alopecia masking lotion normally lasts three to four months.

Topical shading

This is a tinted pressed powder used to cover the scalp in thinning areas and coat hair strands to create a fuller look. The powder is dabbed onto the scalp by using a sponge-tipped applicator, just like applying eye shadow.

✂

The manufacturers of camouflaging products highlight that they will not block pores or interfere with normal hair growth. Links are on the Halo website (see p. 147) for places where you can purchase them online or by mail order.

Camouflaging tips

- ✂ For oily to normal skin on the scalp use a pressed powder as this is absorbed well and prevents a shiny scalp.
- ✂ For dry to normal skin on the scalp use a cream to prevent dryness.
- ✂ Choose the product that is least likely to wipe off. You can test this by applying the product to the back of your hand, allowing it to dry for five minutes, then wiping the area with a damp cloth. If it doesn't come off then it's a good one!
- ✂ Fibres need hairs to bind to, so people with advanced hair loss do better with sprays and creams. Try different products with a friend to see which is best for you.

HAIR REPLACEMENTS

A change in hairstyle or camouflaging measures may not meet the needs of women who have moderate to severe hair loss. In these cases an integration, a hairpiece, or a wig may be an option.

There have been many advances in hair replacement over the past ten years. Hair extensions are now choices for women with mild hair loss who simply desire more length and volume. Extensions can be clipped on daily or attached permanently to your hair. They are not suitable, however, for women who have hair that breaks off easily because of their weight and because they can sometimes damage your hair when not applied correctly. So if you are considering extensions, ask your hairdresser for a recommendation, or contact an alopecia support group (see pp. 147–8).

Integrations

Integrations work in conjunction with your natural hair by complementing it and adding volume. They may be suitable for you whether you have lost a little or a lot of hair from the top of the head, just as long as you still have areas of healthy hair in other places on the scalp. Your own hair from the thinning areas is blended with that of the integration. The result is the appearance of a full head of hair.

An integration is made of fabric or skin-like material that has replacement hair attached to it and gaps through which you pull your own hair. It can be secured with bobby pins, clips, combs, double-sided tape, or fused to your existing hair. You can wear it daily or for extended periods, although it's recommended you remove it before bed to extend its life and prevent scalp irritations.

The attached hair can be synthetic or human. Human hair provides a more natural look and tends to last longer. However, the integration's life mostly depends on how well you care for it. If you can afford it, it is a good idea to get two. That way you will always have one on hand.

> **Pro** — an integration incorporates your own hair, resulting in a full and more natural-looking head of hair.

> **Con** — it can cause stress to your existing hair, resulting in damage and hair breakage. If worn for extended periods it can cause scalp irritations.

If your hair loss is extensive and your remaining hair cannot tolerate an integration you can opt for a hairpiece or full wig.

Hairpieces

Hairpieces are one step above integrations. They consist of skin-like, breathable material that holds the attached hair securely in place and are designed to be worn twenty-four hours a day. You can wake up in the morning with a full head of hair! Hairpieces are usually attached to the scalp by adhesive tape, but they may be attached by hair clips, so you can remove the piece at the end of the day if you choose.

Hairpieces are generally made to match your scalp tone and existing hair texture and colour. This attention to detail provides a natural appearance and allows you to move your head without you feeling uncomfortable or self-conscious about your scalp being exposed. They are placed only on the areas of the scalp that are thinning and can cover both small and larger areas of hair loss.

Wigs

If your hair loss is in the advanced stage, the next option is a wig. A wig can provide a high level of security without limiting your usual activities, be they working out at the gym, swimming or going out on a windy day. With a good quality, well-fitted wig, you'll regain the appearance of full hair and boost your self-esteem.

Wigs come in many sizes, styles, textures and colours. They can be machine or custom-made and are available in both synthetic fibres and human hair. The wig base (to which the hairs are attached) can be polyester, polyurethane, nylon or silicone.

Machine versus custom-made

Machine-made wigs consist of wefts of hair sewn together by machine; the hair is generally not altered apart from curl and style once selected. It takes from three to six weeks to create a machine-made wig.

Custom-made wigs are designed to look as natural as possible. A wig-maker takes either a detailed measurement or a cast of your head, and hand-ties synthetic or human hair to a wig base that's matched to the skin tone of your scalp. These wigs are securely attached to the scalp using one of several methods including adhesive tape, the 'tight fit' method, or a suction attachment. They take from three weeks to six months to prepare and vary in price enormously, depending on the type of materials used — particularly the hair — and quality.

Synthetic versus human hair

Synthetic wigs have improved over the years in style, colour, texture and quality and are more natural looking than ever before. They cost less than human hair wigs and retain their style well, but apart from cutting, the style cannot be changed. You should also avoid applying styling products such as mousse and hairspray to your synthetic wig as they may damage and reduce its life. You should keep in mind that heat can melt the synthetic fibres in these wigs, so avoid cooking while wearing your synthetic wig!

Human hair is stunning and, if carefully chosen and well-made, looks as natural as your own. When you are tired of your old style or colour, you can change either without getting a new wig. You can also use styling products such as hair spray on it. Depending how you look after it, your human hair wig will last much longer than a synthetic one, but there's a drawback — it's far more expensive.

When considering a human hair wig, be sure to ask the wig-maker the following questions: is the hair to be used in your wig Caucasian, Asian or African? Is the hair naturally straight or wavy? These hair characteristics may not be apparent from samples you are shown and can have a significant impact on the colouring, styling and perming potential of your new wig. A reputable wig-maker will be able to tell you where the hair has come from, how it has been treated since leaving the original owner's head and the costs associated with the various characteristics.

Wig care

Unlike your own hair, wigs are relatively easy to care for.

Synthetic wigs can be shampooed and placed on a wig stand to dry naturally with minimal care. Human hair wigs require more attention than synthetic wigs. Before washing, brush the hair gently but completely. Wash the wig in cold water using a gentle shampoo and conditioner. Gently squeeze out excess water and blot the wig with towel. Next, place it on a clean dry towel and allow it to dry naturally.

Whether your wig is made of synthetic or human hair, you should follow the wig-maker's specific instructions on how to care for it. Sometimes, this may include returning your wig to the wig-maker on a regular basis for specialist care.

This is a bit like taking your car in for a regular service and tune; it will prolong the life and condition of your investment.

Before you buy

Before you purchase a hair replacement, there are several things you need to do and consider:

- ✂ Explore all options, and shop around. There are companies that specialise in designing wigs for people with hair loss conditions.
- ✂ Contact an alopecia support group (see pp. 147–8) for advice on finding an experienced wig maker who is sensitive to your needs.
- ✂ Try on wigs with different styles, lengths and colours.
- ✂ Find out the various costs associated with your intended purchase, including preparation and maintenance costs.
- ✂ If you are still uncertain about which type of hair replacement to buy, or unsure whether you will feel comfortable wearing one at all, consider purchasing a less expensive wig until you work out what best suits you.
- ✂ Take a trusted family member or friend with you to provide honest advice and support.

HAIR ACCESSORIES AND ADDITIONS

If you feel uncomfortable about the idea of purchasing an integration or a wig but would like to cover your thinning hair, there are alternatives.

Fashion accessories to conceal your hair problem come in the form of hats, scarves, bandanas and turbans that are available in many colours, textures and styles.

Hair additions can be combs and headbands with hair attached to them, ponytails that easily attach to your existing hair, and hair scrunchies. You can have a lot of fun with these and match your style with your mood. Perhaps you can be creative and design your own head coverings to use as a fashion statement when going to a special event, or for more low-key activities such as gardening.

WHEN IT HAPPENED TO ME ...
Sabrina, 58

Sabrina's life turned upside down when her husband died. Her hair had been thin most of her life, but she'd always managed to coax it into looking presentable. When her hair began to look noticeably thinner, she put it down to stress.

After her husband's death, the thinning became so bad she visited a dermatologist. At her first appointment, her dermatologist was able to confirm that she had female pattern hair loss. Sabrina sought a second opinion, which yielded the same result. She fled the second dermatologist's office with her head spinning. The loss of her husband compounded by the idea that she probably would have no hair left in a couple of months was devastating.

Sabrina tried to come to terms with this latest challenge in her life by searching for solutions. First, she visited a wig salon.

> It left me an emotional mess. At the time I was looking for solace, yet the way the saleswoman treated me, I could have been looking for a piece of furniture. So I turned to a kind woman who made fashion wigs for women in the Jewish community instead.

With this woman's help, Sabrina picked out a wig which was similar to a hairstyle she'd worn when she was younger.

STYLING, CAMOUFLAGING AND REPLACING

'I was quite excited as I drove home, imagining how my friends and family would react to my new look.'

At first the wig remained on its stand like a goal post she wasn't yet ready to reach. A couple of months passed and by the time she did summon the courage to wear it, she realised her hair wasn't thinning at the rate she'd thought it would. On the few occasions she did put it on, people complimented her.

'Most people didn't even seem to realise it wasn't my own.'

Yet the wig soon found its way back onto its stand, permanently.

> Yes, it looked great on me, though it tended to slip at times. But that didn't bother me too much. The real problem was that wearing a wig somehow seemed to change who I was. It wasn't me!

At that point Sabrina looked in the mirror and decided she would simply accept and cope with gradual hair loss.

Three years later Sabrina changed her mind again. She looked at her severely thinning hair and felt the same as she had about the wig.

'I no longer looked like myself.'

She found it harder to conceal her thinning hair and became very self-conscious. Two years ago, she decide to commence treatment with the anti-androgen, spironolactone.

> At first the medication didn't seem to do anything, but recently the hair loss seems to be slowing down. I go through various stages of accepting my hair looking very thin, and times when I feel that old shame and embarrassment. But I no longer feel the need to sit in the back row of meetings, or cover my hair with a scarf, hat or beret.

Sabrina has discovered a hairdresser who specialises in cutting hair for women with hair loss, and who is able to make her hair seem fuller. She has also bought a less expensive synthetic wig which suits her face and age. She wears it from time to time when she knows she might feel self-conscious, particularly on special occasions.

> I accept my hair isn't my crowning glory. I've told my friends and my work colleagues about it and have found them

> sympathetic. I count my blessings —
> satisfying work as a teacher, a healthy
> family, good friends. Thinning hair doesn't
> interfere with my bushwalking and other
> pleasures, such as reading and socialising.
> Over the seven years I've been single I've
> been on many dates. None of the men
> appeared to have a problem with my thin
> hair.

Sabrina has learnt to use make-up more competently in order to make her eyes more dramatic. Belonging to a support group has also been a great help.

> I've learned courage by example through
> the women in the group whose hair loss is
> more serious than mine. I've shared my
> fears and have sympathised with others'
> stories. Most importantly, I've found a
> way to cope by realising I'm not alone.

7
Myths and medical treatments

Historical records reveal many questionable treatments that make it clear the extraordinary — and ultimately ineffectual lengths — to which people would go to stop their hair loss.

In 1585 Humphrey Lloyd suggested, 'Burn the head of a large rat and mingle it with the dropping of a bear or of a hog and anoint the head. It heals the disease called Alopecia.'

Rubbing goose or dove droppings into your scalp will not cure your hair loss, either. And neither will going to bed with a mixture of bull's blood and semen slapped over the scalp and covered with a towel.

BEWARE TODAY!

Some modern, if cleaner and less pungent actions and advice can be equally useless.

Remember, hair is only alive *inside* the hair follicle. Once it grows up through the scalp it's dead and this means that cutting your hair:

- ✂ will *not* make it grow thicker
- ✂ will *not* make it grow faster
- ✂ will *not* make it healthier
- ✂ will have *no effect* whatsoever, except to make it shorter — but you knew that.

Don't try standing on your head, either, in the hope it will increase blood flow and somehow reduce hair loss. It won't.

✂

Since your hair is dead by the time you see it, no product, no matter what the label says, can make your hair healthier, stronger, thicker, denser or longer. Numerous products for hair loss are sold over the counter. Although their ingredients are generally safe for external use, they neither promote hair growth nor prevent hair loss. In 1980 the United States Food and Drug Administration

(FDA) evaluated a number of substances used in hair lotions and creams, and subsequently proposed the hair products containing them be removed from the market. The substances included amino acids, aminobenzoic acid, ascorbic acid, benzoic acid, B vitamins, hormones, jojoba oil, lanolin, polysorbates 20 and 660, sulfanilimide, tetracaine hydrochloride, urea and wheatgerm oil.

Other ineffective remedies for FPHL include scalp massage, dietary modification, iron and zinc supplements, electrical stimulation, laser combs and Chinese herbal extracts.

While not specifically mentioned by the FDA, laser treatments have recently been promoted as a means to stimulate hair growth. Many laser therapy centres claim fantastic results and refer to in-house data. In fact very little information about these devices has been published, and what is available is very soft science. The authors are not convinced laser therapy has anything to offer women who are losing their hair.

Saw palmetto is a herbal extract that partially inhibits conversion of testosterone to DHT. This is how finasteride works in treating male pattern hair loss, however the effect of saw palmetto is much weaker. Even if you had a bottle a day of saw palmetto you would be unlikely to regrow even half as much as someone taking finasteride.

However, chemical treatments such as bleaching, tinting and straightening, and heat treatments such as blow-drying on the highest setting, or the use of curling irons or straightening tongs can all damage the structure and condition of your *visible* hair if they are not applied correctly, or if the frequency, timing or concentrations are wrong.

HEADING FOR TREATMENT

Most people with dermatological problems such as psoriasis, eczema or acne don't think twice about starting medical treatment promptly. Yet six months or even a year may pass before a woman seeks help for losing her hair. During that time she may have put the loss down to stress, hormonal changes, the weather or illness.

This first year is critical. The sooner appropriate treatment is started, the better the results in the long term.

The three principle aims are to:

1. Arrest further progression

2. Stimulate hair regrowth

3. Conceal the hair loss

Most treatments achieve only two out of three goals.

Topical minoxidil stimulates regrowth but may or may not arrest further progression, at least in the long term.

Anti-androgen tablets such as **spironolactone** and **cyproterone acetate** appear to halt further progression, and may stimulate regrowth in some women. They block the effect of androgen hormones and can be taken on their own or while minoxidil is being applied. Research shows hair loss is halted in over ninety per cent of women who use oral anti-androgens, while about thirty to forty per cent experience some regrowth. Women are advised not to become pregnant while taking anti-androgen medication.

Hair transplantation redistributes the hair more evenly over the scalp, but does not arrest further hair loss. It works on the principal of robbing Peta to pay Pauline, taking hair from the back of the head and redistributing it over the crown to create the illusion of more hair. It is less useful for diffuse thinning over the crown, and generally women with severe FPHL who have completely bald areas on the top of their scalp are the only ones who opt for it. However, micrograft hair transplantation can be used for some women with diffuse hair loss that is advanced, as long as they have thick hair at the back of the scalp that can be taken and transplanted. It may take six to nine months before the full benefit of the transplant can be seen.

MINOXIDIL LOTION

Minoxidil is a hair growth lotion that is applied directly to the scalp and may be used alone or in combination with the anti-androgen tablets. Minoxidil halts further hair loss, and stimulates mild to moderate hair regrowth in approximately sixty per cent of women.

No one is entirely sure how minoxidil works. We do know it increases the duration of the anagen (growth) phase of the hair cycle which means hairs grow longer, and it shortens the duration of the telogen (resting) phase of the cycle which leads to fewer empty follicles on the scalp. It may also increase the thickness of the individual strands of hair. The result of all this is a reduction in hair shedding and an increase in hair density on the areas where it's been applied.

Minoxidil lotion comes in two strengths: five per cent and two per cent. The greatest hair growth occurs after six months of continuous, once-a-day use of the five per cent lotion; the same effect may take up to twelve months to achieve using the two per cent lotion, twice a day.

You need to use minoxidil lotion continuously (every day) to maintain hair regrowth. When it's used for twelve months and then stopped, the scalp returns to its the pre-treatment state and all the hair that regrew with minoxidil is shed, but no additional hair is lost. It's not yet known if women who have used minoxidil lotion for many years and then stop will lose all the hairs regrown with minoxidil.

MAKING TREATMENT EASIER

Applying the five per cent solution once a day only, each night, and washing it off each morning is less time consuming. It also decreases the chances of side effects and is cheaper than using two per cent minoxidil twice a day.

Having to apply the two per cent solution twice a day doubles the effort involved, costs more, and in the morning can make hair greasy and difficult to style just when you're getting ready to leave for work, hurry to an appointment or meet friends.

ARE THERE SIDE EFFECTS?

There is the potential for side effects when using minoxidil, just as there is with any medication.

Perhaps the most frequently reported one is the appearance of unwanted hair in places other than the scalp — usually on the forehead. The reason for this is probably in part the minoxidil being absorbed into the skin and having a regional effect, and in part some of the solution running down onto the forehead. Any hair that appears on the forehead will go away once the minoxidil is stopped, or sometimes reducing the strength of minoxidil to two per cent, or applying less solution, is enough to make unwanted hair disappear. A depilatory cream can be helpful. Some women are pleased with the result on their scalp and not too worried by the hair on their forehead.

About ten per cent of women who use minoxidil

lotion get scalp irritation (itch or dandruff). In general the irritation is mild and daily use of an anti-dandruff shampoo is enough to deal with it. These shampoos generally have conditioning agents and are safe for everyday use.

If the irritation is severe, you might find tar-based shampoos helpful. These and similar products are available from pharmacies. Some women will also benefit from a prescription for cortisone lotion that they can apply to the scalp. You will need to ask your doctor for this.

If you do not get relief from irritation using any of the above strategies, you should discuss using the weaker two per cent minoxidil lotion with your doctor or pharmacist.

The impact of minoxidil on unborn babies is not known, so discuss your plans to have children with your doctor before becoming pregnant. There is no evidence that using minoxidil affects women's ability to conceive or carry to full term.

WHICH BRAND OF MINOXIDIL?

Originally minoxidil lotion was available as two per cent Rogaine. The five per cent lotion was developed about fifteen years ago and is sold as Rogaine Extra Strength. It was difficult for scientists to formulate the stronger solution, and it took about ten years to achieve stabilisation in the bottle for even dispersal over the scalp.

The production of generic minoxidil solutions for sale in Australia is regulated by the Therapeutic Goods Administration (TGA) to ensure they contain correct concentrations of the active ingredient. However, almost all the available scientific data on effectiveness is related to Rogaine specifically and may or may not be applicable to the generic lotions as the TGA does not require bioequivalence testing[1] for approval of generic products.

APPLICATION OF MINOXIDIL

Here is what we suggest:
- Use five per cent minoxidil once a day, in the evening only.
- Apply the five per cent minoxidil after you have finished the day's activities (e.g. been to

---

[1] Bioequivalence testing means testing for an equivalent biological effect.

the gym, out to dinner, visiting) and are winding down for the evening.

✂ Apply the product to your dry hair as described on the packaging.

✂ Let your hair dry completely before hopping into bed. This will help prevent the product rubbing off onto your sheets and pillow and then onto your face.

✂ In the morning wash, condition and style your hair as usual.

✂ Change your pillow cases daily. This will ensure that any product that does accidentally end up on your pillow does not build up and find its way back onto you.

✂ Include minoxidil application in your nightly beauty routine — this will greatly reduce the impact of treatment on your day-to-day life. And no one else need know about it!

PICTURING PROGRESS

One reason women may feel like giving up on their treatment is because they can't tell whether or not it's working. Often they find it difficult to judge what's happening on top of their head. Scalp photographs are very helpful. We recommend women have photographs of their scalp taken by a trained medical photographer before they commence treatment and every six months thereafter to monitor their progress.

If a professional medical photography service is not available near you, you can try taking them yourself, although it can be difficult to assess through a home photo if the treatment is working.

PHOTOGRAPHING YOUR SCALP

1. Photograph your hair 24 hours or more after washing it.
2. The best lighting is natural lighting.
3. The camera and head positions should be similar each time.
4. If you dye your hair always take the photo within a week or two of colouring it.
5. Part your hair neatly in the centre and hold it flat.

TESTING PROGRESS

Another way to judge whether minoxidil lotion is working is to stop after you have been using it continuously for twelve months. If you notice increased hair shedding four to six weeks later, the treatment definitely was effective. You should go straight back on it and continue it for life.

Not all women who use minoxidil experience regrowth, but their hair loss may have been halted. Halting further loss is an important goal, and so we only recommend women stop using the lotion if they have been on it longer than twelve months and feel certain their overall hair density is worse. Persistent hair shedding does not necessarily mean minoxidil is not working.

THE EARLY STAGE OF TREATMENT

When women first start using minoxidil their hair shedding sometimes increases. This is due to resting telogen hair follicles being stimulated to start growing again, and the new hairs subsequently pushing dead telogen hairs out of the follicle. This shedding generally only lasts a few weeks and is often mild. When it's severe, women usually panic — the lotion that is supposed to be stopping hair loss is actually making things worse! The good news is that if you continue the treatment, the shedding slows and then stops. In fact, the women who experience the most severe temporary shedding are the ones who get the best hair regrowth in the long term.

While an increase in shedding isn't necessary for regrowth, those who do temporarily worsen simply need to keep their nerve and continue the treatment for at least six months to see the benefit.

WHEN IT HAPPENED TO ME ...
Heather, 35

Heather first noticed that she was losing more hair than usual about four years ago. It was after a traumatic time in her life, so she first put it down to stress, as did the two doctors she saw. One dismissed her worries and distress and recommended she consider taking antidepressants.

> This was five minutes into the consultation when the doctor knew absolutely nothing about my situation and concerns. I was furious and stormed out!

Heather is no stranger to female hair loss. Her mother had experienced bouts of alopecia areata (a condition where hair falls out in patches). On her father's side, she has three aunts who have suffered female pattern hair loss for years and a female cousin who, at thirty, was diagnosed with alopecia universalis (a condition where all hair is lost on the scalp and body).

After experiencing several weeks of severe shedding, Heather sought professional help.

'I was scared and devastated and couldn't believe this was also happening to me. I just wanted my hair back.'

Heather felt powerless to stop her hair from falling out. She became so self-conscious about her hair thinning she soon became less social and withdrawn. 'I couldn't bear to look at my hair in the mirror.'

She decided to see a dermatologist who specialises in hair loss conditions and diseases. To add to her distress, there was a seven month waiting list.

'Are you kidding?' Heather said to the secretary. 'There is no way that I can wait that long. My hair will be gone by then!'

Heather's distress and frustration soon changed to desperation. She sought the help of natural remedies such as vitamins, herbs, hair loss prevention lotions and tablets to treat her hair loss.

> I happened to walk by a Chinese medicine clinic and there was a sign saying 'Treatment for hair loss here!' I immediately made an appointment and the following day saw a doctor who claimed my hair would stop falling out after three weeks of taking a herbal remedy. So that evening I boiled the herbs but struggled to swallow the mixture because it smelt and tasted revolting. I was told to take the mixture three times a week for six to twelve months, so for the sake of my hair I would block my nose and drink up! After a couple of months, I had to stop because more often than not I would throw up. I couldn't take the mixture any more!

After exploring various alternative treatments to hair loss, Heather eventually saw the dermatologist who took a biopsy and

MYTHS AND MEDICAL TREATMENTS

diagnosed her condition as female pattern hair loss. She learnt that her condition was hereditary, progressive and common in women her age, that she had already lost thirty per cent of her hair density but medical treatment would put a stop to further hair loss.

Heather left the initial consultation in tears yet relieved to finally know she was suffering from a specific hair loss condition and not going crazy. She could now share this information with family and friends where she hoped to get the support and understanding she needed. She started medical treatment but was concerned that she had to be on medication indefinitely.

The following year Heather experienced many ups and downs related to her hair thinning. She still had periods of hair shedding and found it difficult to come to terms with her condition. Even though she had frequently heard her balding aunt say, 'I would be a happier person, if only I had my hair,' Heather never imagined how bad her aunt had felt about it. Until now.

Her self-confidence and self-esteem were at

their lowest. She constantly thought about her hair loss, which made her feel sad. She felt guilty because she was allowing her hair loss to take over her life — it was affecting her work performance, her social activities and her relationship with her partner.

> I thought I was silly to feel this way because there were illnesses in the world much worse than hair loss, but still for a woman, losing her hair was just not right!

Heather shared her distress with her dermatologist. He suggested she see a psychologist trained in assisting people with hair loss conditions (see p. 148). Initially Heather resisted seeking counselling. She felt guilty about needing support for a condition that wasn't life-threatening.

> After attending the first session I wondered whether I'd benefit from continuing because it forced me to think about my hair and I found that too confronting. But continuing with the therapy was the most beneficial thing I ever did for my hair! The psychologist was understanding and supportive, and

provided me with the skills to cope better with my condition. My self-esteem and self-confidence improved along with my relationship with my partner and work colleagues.

8
Planning and patience

After diagnosis some women experience a period of resistance to starting treatment because they aren't quite ready to accept the condition as part of their lives, their daily routine and their identity. This is a completely natural reaction, and if you feel like this it doesn't mean you're being a difficult patient. Keep in mind, though, if you begin the application of minoxidil in the early stages of the condition, you are more likely to hang on to your healthy hair follicles, slow down hair loss, and regrow hair.

It's very important you feel ready for treatment before you begin it, to ensure you give yourself the best chance of staying the distance. You need to consider the following points:

- ✂ Am I ready to accept the diagnosis?
- ✂ Will the treatment really make a difference?
- ✂ Will the treatment fit in with my lifestyle?
- ✂ Are there side effects? (see p. 112)
- ✂ What will happen if I stop treatment? (see p. 111)

Deciding to start treatment for your hair loss is a big step. It means making a big mental shift from, 'It might not be female pattern hair loss … my hair loss might be temporary and it might thicken up on its own,' to, 'Okay. I've been examined by my doctor and it *is* female pattern hair loss. What do I want to do about it?'

PERSONAL HELP

If you haven't done so already, consider telling somcone you trust what you're about to embark on. You've probably worked hard to conceal your condition from those around you, perhaps even from your immediate family. Having a confidante can be a great outlet, particularly at bad times.

Developing self-relaxation techniques will also

be important as you prepare yourself to begin treatment. There are going to be good days and bad days, and you want to be ready for anything. Some simple techniques for relaxing and managing upsetting thoughts are provided on p. 135.

Prepare for the possibility of additional hair loss that occurs to about one in three women during the first six months of treatment by asking yourself the following:

- ✂ When will be the best time to start treatment?
- ✂ What will I be doing at work, home and with the family?
- ✂ Will the weather be hot or cold?
- ✂ Do I have holidays or other special events planned?
- ✂ How will I manage this phase?

You can avoid a lot of stress associated with sudden increased hair loss by planning ahead and discussing your options with your doctor. If you plan to wear hats to conceal the extra loss, you might prefer to start treatment as the cooler weather starts. If you plan to go on holiday, move house or expect to be under stress at work in the next six months, you should discuss how this will affect your treatment because you don't want to put yourself under any more pressure than is absolutely necessary.

Treatment with minoxidil is a long, hard road, but if you stick with it you are likely to have success. It should make no more of an impact on your day-to-day life than any other part of your beauty routine. Think of it as just another product like your moisturiser, hair fudge or cleanser that takes only a few minutes to apply. Plan ahead if you are travelling and ensure you have a continuous supply.

DON'T WONDER AND WORRY ... ASK!

Doctors aren't qualified mind-readers. They won't know what you're thinking or wondering about, or how you're feeling, unless you tell them. It's very important that you make a note of any questions or concerns you have and raise them at your next appointment. Don't imagine you are being stupid or a nuisance or a bad patient.

Let your doctor know if:

✂ you are confused or unsure about something

- you were told at a previous appointment, or by your pharmacist, or by another doctor
- you are having trouble maintaining your treatment
- you have stopped your medication for any reason
- you are experiencing severe scalp irritation

AS THE MONTHS GO BY

You might want to keep a simple diary. Not the Bridget Jones type, but a small notebook in which you can write your questions. Note how the treatment affects your mood and thoughts and day-to-day life and track how your hair is reacting to the treatment.

Your commitment will be tested in the first months particularly if you are one of those who experience temporary shedding. This early increased and rapid hair loss is a sign the treatment is working. It means new, healthier hair is on its way.

There is always a delay of between three and six months from starting minoxidil to seeing new hair. This effect is well known and is a normal part of successful treatment.

Being prepared for possible extra loss and knowing your condition is *not* deteriorating will lessen the impact. It might be a good time to start experimenting with scarves, hats[2], camouflage or accessories, and you might need to take extra time with your hairstyling during this period. But remember, your hair will improve in time.

Patience is going to be your best resource during the first year. Some women become disheartened. They feel the minoxidil isn't working and are tempted to give up. Although twelve months might seem like a long time, remember that normal scalp hairs generally grow for between two and five years, then rest for around three months before naturally falling out.

How well the treatment will work will depend on a number of factors including your general health, the severity of your hair loss, and how closely you adhere to the regime. And remember the deck of cards — your genes. We can put the handbrake on FPHL, but we can't re-shuffle the pack.

---

[2] See 'Styling, camouflaging and replacing' on p. 83.

WHEN IT HAPPENED TO ME …
Nicole, 42

Nicole started to notice her hair was shedding in her early twenties, but she didn't pay much attention to it. She thought it was probably due to stress in her personal life and soon would pass. It didn't occur to her it might be a hereditary condition.

She saw a number of doctors, both general practitioners and specialists, who provided her with information she didn't find helpful. Eventually she was told she was suffering from female pattern hair loss, similar to male pattern baldness, that she'd most likely inherited from her parents.

Nicole was horrified, confused and angry this had happened to her. She thought male pattern baldness occurred only to males.

> I was upset with this diagnosis and the specialist's lack of compassion and disregard for my feelings. He offered me a course of medication I would need to take indefinitely, with little hope for improvement.

Nicole found that there was little information available and little known about her condition. She trawled books, the media and the Internet. She purchased many products advertised to help people with hair loss, even though she knew a cure was not something she could buy. As her loss of hair became more apparent, it became more difficult for her to deal with it.

Nicole has now been receiving medical treatment (cyproterone acetate and minoxidil) for ten years, with breaks of six months to a year. When she took a break from treatment, she did notice changes to her hair, and she experienced more hair shedding for four months after ceasing her medications.

> It's hard to observe any real difference when taking medication, but once you stop, the shedding is more noticeable. Sometimes I feel depressed and helpless but for most of the time I try to get on with my life.
>
> Accepting my condition has been difficult, but knowing that I'm doing the best I can to help my condition is

PLANNING AND PATIENCE

comforting. After years of soul searching, I finally realised I'm a special person and having hair loss shouldn't limit me from doing the things I want to do.

Appendix
Techniques for relaxation

To receive the maximum benefit from these techniques, you need to practise them regularly. Each day make time once for a progressive muscle relaxation, and several times for practising the controlled breathing technique. You might want to stick reminders around the place so you don't forget. You could buy a pack of small, adhesive gold or silver stars (like the ones that teachers put on children's school work) and stick one on your mobile phone, inside your draw or locker at work, in your purse, on the dashboard of your car — anywhere that will catch your eye and prompt you to take thirty seconds to relax.

After a week or two of regular relaxation sessions, you'll discover as you settle down to relax, you'll *already* feel yourself relaxing. This is because your mind and body have come to expect that when you sit in this particular chair, at this particular time, you'll end up relaxed. In time, you'll find that just thinking about relaxing will make you relaxed!

Interestingly, acting as though you're relaxed makes you relaxed.

GOOD TIMES AND PLACES

- ✂ When you have at least half an hour where you won't be interrupted.
- ✂ A time you don't need to do something else.
- ✂ A location you can access regularly. Eventually you'll find the place itself becomes associated with relaxation.

POOR TIMES AND PLACES

- ✂ After a meal. Your body is busy digesting food and you might need to go to the toilet in the middle of the session. A big meal might make you sleepy, too, and falling asleep doesn't have the same benefits as deep relaxation.

✂ In bed. Your bed is for sleeping and sex *only*.

✂ When you have something else that needs to be done. Making time to relax is important but don't schedule a session at the same time as another planned activity, for example, when you would usually help your son with his homework. Double booking may increase your anxiety and lead to an association between practising relaxation and becoming even more stressed!

PROGRESSIVE MUSCLE RELAXATION

This technique involves sitting or lying in a quiet, low-lit location of your choice and — one by one — becoming aware of, tensing, and then relaxing each of your major muscle groups. As you practise you'll be surprised at the amount of tension held in your muscles and joints and the depth of relaxation you can achieve by becoming aware of your body.

Below is a suggestion for the order of muscle relaxation, starting at your toes and ending at the top of your head. Left-handers may want to start on the left side of their body while others may prefer to start with the scalp and work their way down. Feel free to adopt the order that best suits you.

Tense and relax:
1. Right foot and toes
2. Left foot and toes
3. Right lower leg and foot
4. Left lower leg and foot
5. Right upper leg
6. Left upper leg
7. Hips
8. Abdomen
9. Chest
10. Shoulders
11. Right upper arm
12. Left upper arm
13. Right forearm and hand
14. Left forearm and hand
15. Right hand and fingers
16. Left hand and fingers
17. Neck
18. Face and head (jaw, eyes and scalp)

There are two methods for progressive muscle relaxation: **unguided** and **guided**.

The **unguided** method involves learning the

eighteen muscle groups listed and working through them at your own pace, in silence or perhaps with some soothing music in the background.

The **guided** method involves relaxing your muscles according to a script such as the one provided below. Many guided relaxation tapes and CDs are available commercially in good book and health stores. You either can have someone read the script to you in a slow, even voice, or you may want to make your own recording (e.g. tape, CD, MP3) of the script that you can listen to through your stereo or headphones. It can be your own voice reading the script or that of a friend or family member.

GUIDED RELAXATION SCRIPT

Take a deep breath ... filling your lungs, right to the bottom. Close your eyes, let your head sink back and begin to relax ... feel yourself relaxing every muscle in your body, from the top of your head ... to the tips of your toes ... Begin to relax and notice just how heavy your body is beginning to feel. You won't fall ... so just let go and relax. Inhale ... and exhale. Listen to your breathing.

Notice how the rhythm of your breathing slows down as you relax ... Notice the sounds around you. Let them pass you by ... send them away ... From now on, whatever you hear will only help you to relax deeper and deeper. As you exhale, you can feel the tension and stress washing away from every part of your body and your mind. With each breath, feel the stress and tension float away.

Notice how the thoughts that trouble you just drift away, further and further, smaller and smaller ... Feel the air on your face ... feel it brushing your face and relaxing the muscles around your mouth and your jaw. Feel your jaw relax as your head sinks deeper and deeper into your pillow. Feel the tension in your jaw wash away with every breath ... feel your skin become heavier and heavier as you fall deeper and deeper into relaxation. Feel the relaxation spread to your temples. Relax the muscles in your temples and feel the heaviness spread to your eyes. Feel the tension fall away from your eyes as the air brushes your eyelids. As you feel your eyelids become heavy, you begin to sink deeper and deeper into relaxation. Now let the tension wash away from your forehead ... and as you do, you feel your skin become smooth and heavy as your muscles relax. Feel the tension wash away with every breath.

And now feel the muscles in your shoulders relax. As you exhale, feel the heavy, heavy weight being lifted from your shoulders. You feel relieved as the tension floats away and your lungs fill with cool, cool air. As the tension floats away from you, the muscles in the back of your neck and shoulders relax, and you sink deeper and deeper ... and you feel the soothing relaxation wash down your spine, down, down, down ... soothing you ... as tension floats away ... down, down, to the base of your spine ... let the muscles go, with every breath you take ... inhale ... exhale. Just feel your body sinking, deeper and deeper, into total relaxation. Let the muscles in your back go ... feel them becoming smooth and heavy, becoming softer and softer ... Notice the muscles in your shoulders ... feel them running down your arms to your fingertips. Feel the tension wash away, from your shoulders, down your arms and to your fingers. Send the tension away ... with every breath ... feel the tension float away from your fingers as you exhale ... as the tension washes away, your arms feel heavy, so relaxed and heavy. Feel the tingle in your fingertips ... the warmth in the palms ... as you send the tension away. You're so relaxed that you can barely lift your arms ... they are so heavy, and so relaxed.

As you inhale once again, you notice your chest muscles ... how they stretch ... and how they relax as you exhale ... You feel your stomach muscles stretch ... and relax ... As you exhale, feel the tension float away from you ... your stomach muscles relax ... Feel the tension fall away from your hips as the feeling of relaxation spreads from your chest down to your thighs ... Let the muscles in your legs go ... all of the muscles in your legs ... let them relax ... feel the relaxation wash down your legs from your thighs ... to your calves ... ankles ... all the way to the tips of your toes. As the waves of relaxation wash over your legs, notice how very heavy your body feels ... just sinking ... deeper, deeper and deeper.

As you relax, deeper and deeper, you find yourself at the top of a beautiful sweeping staircase. There are only ten steps down ... and the steps lead you to a warm, peaceful place ... A place that is very special to you ... Soon, you will step gently ... and slowly, down the staircase and enter that special place ... I am going to count backward from ten to one. As I count, you will descend the staircase ... and with each step you take, you will feel your body relax, more and more and more ... feel yourself drifting down, down ... relaxing you deeper and deeper and deeper.

10 ... relaxing deeper ... 9 ... 8 ... 7 ... 6 ... 5 ... 4 ... 3 ... 2 ... 1 ... deeper and deeper and deeper.

And now you are in a warm, peaceful and special place. You can feel the warmth of the breeze as it brushes your body ... washing away your worries ... You are all alone ... in solitude ... there is no one here to disturb you ... This is the most peaceful place in the world for you ... you feel a sense of peace flow through you ... of wellbeing ... enjoy this pleasurable feeling and keep it with you long after you return home ... keep this feeling for the rest of the day ... into the evening ... and tomorrow. Allow these pleasurable feelings to grow stronger and stronger ... filling you with a sense of peace, of wellbeing ... and every time you come back to this place, you will relax deeper and deeper and deeper. In this place, your worries just float away on the breeze ... leaving you more at peace ... more calm ... more relaxed ... All of your worries just float away on the breeze ... And this pleasurable feeling will stay with you and grow stronger ... and stronger throughout the day as you continue to relax deeper and deeper.

Enjoy the warmth and peace of this special place for a moment ... Then return to the foot of the staircase ... Soon I will begin to count from one to ten. And as I count from one to ten, you will begin to climb the staircase, returning home ... and you will come back feeling refreshed, as though you have had a long restful sleep ... you'll return feeling peaceful ... and relaxed ... Begin to come back now ... place your foot on the first step ... 1 ... 2 ... coming up ... 3 ... 4 ... 5 ... 6 ... feel your eyelids become light once more ... 7 ... 8 ... inhale ... 9 ... exhale ... begin to open your eyes ... 10 ... and you're home.

CONTROLLED BREATHING TECHNIQUE

Controlled breathing techniques help you to reduce anxiety quickly, any place, any time. It's useful just before you walk into a meeting, get up to make a presentation or prepare for a night out. No one will know you are doing it and it takes only about thirty seconds.

The first step is to become aware of your breathing. Is it rapid and shallow? Are you breathing with your chest (your chest puffs out and your shoulders rise with each breath) rather than your diaphragm? The diaphragm is a flat muscle that lies between your lungs and your stomach. When stressed, the diaphragm can become very tense causing you to breathe less deeply. Controlled breathing will train you to breathe from the bottom of your lungs, right down at the diaphragm.

How do you know when you're diaphragm breathing?

Your shoulders and chest remain more or less still but your tummy, just below the ribs, will expand with each inhalation. To feel the difference between chest and diaphragm breathing, place one hand on your chest and one just below your ribs. First take a chest breath, filling up the top of your chest. You'll notice your chest pushes forward and your shoulders rise to make room. Now take a diaphragm breath by attempting to fill the bottom of your lungs with air. You'll notice that your tummy expands to make room for the air and that you can take more air in.

Now you know how to breathe correctly, it's time to learn *controlled* breathing. Take a moment to become aware of your breath and lungs.

In to the count of five.

Let your lungs fill, right to the bottom. As you draw in air, say to yourself, 'In'.

Hold the inhaled air to the count of three.

Breathe *out* to the count of five.

Slowly exhale to the count while saying to yourself, 'Relax.'

Rest for the count of two.

Repeat inhaling, holding and breathing out three times in a row and notice the effect it has on your heart rate and muscle tension. You'll be surprised at the effect it has.

You may choose to substitute the exhale word for something that has a personal meaning to you, for example, 'Peace', 'I am calm', 'drift away'. As you inhale and exhale, concentrate completely on the words you have chosen. Remember George's dad on *Seinfeld*? Serenity *now*!

Useful resources

INFORMATION AND SUPPORT

The Halo Program
www.halo.org.au (see information on the Halo Program on p. 153)

**Alopecia Support Association
(Victoria, Australia)**
Phone: +61 (0)3 9513 8580
home.vicnet.net.au/~aasa

**Women's Androgenetic Support Group
(San Francisco, USA)**
www.heralopecia.com
Click through 'Information' to androgenetic alopecia.

Hair Loss Counselling Service (Victoria, Australia)
Sebastiana Biondo
Skin and Cancer Foundation
Phone: +61 (0)3 9639 1744
Mobile: 0419 398 389
Email: sbiondo@skincancer.asn.au
www.skincancer.asn.au

Anxiety Disorders Association of Victoria
www.adavic.org

DermWeb
www.derm.ubc.ca

Hair loss patient guide
www.hairlosspatientguide.com

keratin.com
www.keratin.com

Patient information
www.womenshairinstitute.com

Rogaine
www.rogaine.com

American Hair Loss Council
www.ahlc.org

HAIR LOSS RESEARCH

Australasian Hair and Wool Research Society
www.ahwrs.org.au

Australasian College of Dermatologists
www.dermcoll.asn.au

European Hair Research Society
www.ehrs.org

Canadian Dermatology Association
www.dermatology.ca

American Academy of Dermatology
www.aad.org

North American Hair Research Society
www.nahrs.org

Oxford Hair Foundation
www.oxfordhairfoundation.org

BOOKS AND ARTICLES

Aisbett, B. *Letting it go: Attaining awareness out of adversity*, HarperCollins, Sydney, 1996.

Aisbett, B. *Living it up: The advanced survivor's guide to anxiety-free living*, HarperCollins, Sydney, 1994.

Aisbett, B. *Living with it: A survivor's guide to panic attacks*, HarperCollins, Sydney, 1993.

Antai-Otong, D. Creative stress management techniques for self-renewal. *Dermatology Nursing* 13(1), 31–39, 2001.

Jacobs, S. *The big fall: Living with hair loss*, Next Century Books, Bedfordshire, 1992.

Kobren, S.D. *The truth about women's hair loss*, McGraw-Hill, Sydney, 2000.

McMullin, R.E. *The new handbook of cognitive therapy techniques*, W.W. Norton, London, 2000.

Montgomery, B., & Evans, L. *You and Stress*, Penguin Books, Melbourne, 1995.

Paul, J. *Solutions to women's hair thinning and loss*, Thomson Delmar Learning, New York, 2005.

Skynner, R., & Cleese, J. *Life and how to survive it*, Mandarin, Melbourne, 1994.

Thompson, W., & Shapiro, J. *Alopecia Areata: Understanding and coping with hair loss*, Johns Hopkins University Press, Baltimore, 2000.

The Halo Program

To promote a better understanding of female pattern hair loss among affected women, the general public, and hair and health professionals we developed the Halo (short for hair loss) Program in 2004. This book is based on it.

The Halo Program is designed specifically for adult women who have been diagnosed by a dermatologist with FPHL, and who are currently receiving, or who are on a waiting list to receive, medical treatment. It provides women with the latest information about their condition, and so complements their medical treatment. It also increases women's ability to persevere with the ongoing treatment.

The program comprises ten weekly sessions, each of two hours. Every meeting consists of two segments: a cognitive-behavioural therapy segment and a practical segment. The main goals are:

- To reduce the negative psychological impact of female pattern hair loss and enhance women's quality of life. The program addresses issues such as low self-esteem, poor body image, low self-confidence, relationship difficulties, anxiety and depression.
- To educate women about coping and relaxation strategies, the nature and course of female pattern hair loss, and treatment options and their efficacy.

Research suggests that some of the difficulties patients have adhering to their treatment can be traced back to poor doctor–patient communication. To this end, the program encourages women to share their own treatment experiences with others, and aims to provide them with the skill and knowledge to speak frankly and with confidence to their doctor.

PARTICIPANTS' COMMENTS
Nicole, 42

The psychological aspects of this condition were never discussed with me by any medical practitioner and so these sessions were very important. They allowed me to express my feelings and fears, and share my experiences in a safe, comfortable and understanding environment.

The program explored the emotional issues associated with female hair loss and provided strategies to deal with them. Being able to cope frees you and changes your perspective, so that you are able to enjoy your life to the fullest.

Michelle, 35

The program will surely help so many women with hair loss who feel as though they are the only people on the planet with this horrible and embarrassing problem!

Sabrina, 58

> The most positive aspect of the course was identifying my negative thoughts and feelings about my hair, and learning ways to control them.

Susanne, 32

> I felt that after the program I gained coping skills and had the tools and insight to move forward.

Jenny, 45

> Including relaxation techniques in the program was helpful. Doing them at home made me feel less anxious about my hair and I was able to stop thinking about it in a negative way.

Julie, 38

> I was hesitant about participating in the program but I'm glad that I did. It provided a safe and comfortable place to share my experiences of hair loss with women who are going through similar issues.

Susanne, 32

It reaches out specifically to women with female pattern hair loss. It was informative — all your questions about the condition, prognosis and treatment are answered.

Belinda, 22

I was recently diagnosed with female pattern hair loss and at the time desperately needed this program in my life. It provided me with support and understanding. I also gained a better understanding about the prognosis and various treatments, and it gave me a sense of hope for the future.

Jenny, 45

I found some of the sessions a little emotionally draining — perhaps from having to confront the subject! I think the informal and friendly atmosphere helped us all to feel comfortable and confident to join in the discussion.

Julie, 38

> I appreciated the flexibility of the program ... I valued the chance to laugh with people about the ridiculous ways we cope with this condition.

Heather, 35

> I attended the Halo Program with a friend who also suffers from female pattern hair loss. I was scared but excited to be sitting in a room with seven other women who were suffering from the same condition. I had so many questions for them — When did you start noticing your hair thinning? How severe is it? How do you feel about it? Are you taking anything for it? If so, is it working? I wanted to know the 'magic potion' to cure my hair problem so I could put it behind me and get on with my life.
>
> The program didn't provide me with a 'magic potion' but it definitely helped me feel better about myself. I valued the fact that we could discuss the problems we were facing in an open and relaxed

environment. I was amazed to see that women of different ages, background, religion, profession and personality experienced similar issues and emotions.